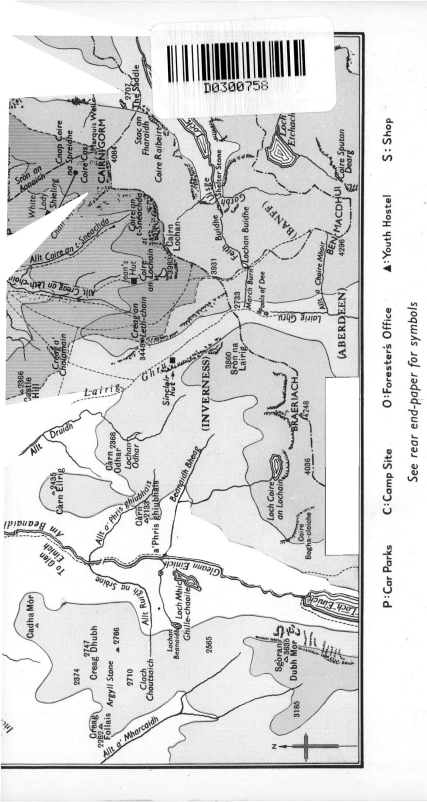

P: Car Parks   C: Camp Site   O: Forester's Office   ▲: Youth Hostel   S: Shop

See rear end-paper for symbols

LOOKING TOWARDS CAIRN LOCHAN FROM THE PASS OF RYVOAN

FOREST PARK GUIDES

GLEN MORE

CAIRNGORMS

Edited by

JOHN WALTON, D.Sc., Sc.D., D.-ès-Sc.,
LL.D., F.R.S.E.

Formerly Regius Professor of Botany in the University of Glasgow
Forestry Commissioner 1949–1954

EDINBURGH
HER MAJESTY'S STATIONERY OFFICE
1966

LOCH MORLICH YOUTH HOSTEL

FOREWORD

By COLONEL JOHN P. GRANT OF ROTHIEMURCHUS

C.B., M.C., T.D., M.A., LL.B., J.P.

WHILE IT is a pleasure to me to write this foreword, this Guide will surely provide its own recommendation to all of those who will take advantage of Glen More as a Forest Park, be they hikers, members of youth clubs, or learned professors of geology, botany or what-not. Every conceivable taste appears to be catered for in this Guide, which has been so ably edited by Professor Walton. For the inexperienced many valuable hints are given by the authors, and I would particularly commend to their attention the few negative hints i.e. the "dont's". If these are well taken to heart we shall hear of fewer accidents, fewer destructive fires, etc. Indeed the time has come for an enlightened public opinion to drive out of business those old pests of the district, professional collectors of rare birds' eggs and rare plants, and to set in their stead the fine new conception of a great Nature Reserve on the Cairngorm Hills.

Those whose interests lie mainly in the articles on the natural history of the Park will be well rewarded by reading, if they have not already done so, Fraser Darling's *Natural History in the Highlands and Islands*. This will give them a clear over-all picture into which the several articles in the Guide fit, and a sense of the interconnection and interaction of the many branches of natural history, such as I have nowhere found so lucidly put. To those of us who inhabit the district it is a humbling experience to be made to realise the vast number of interesting things among which we have lived in blissful ignorance.

I have also had the privilege of watching the growth of the plan for training in outdoor recreation, fathered by the Scottish Council for Physical Recreation, which has given to so many young people from our cities an opportunity to enjoy their heritage of hills, forests and lochs. For at Glen More Lodge, now re-housed in excellent modern premises, we have a centre for the training of men and women interested in outdoor life, who are able and willing to pass on their skill and knowledge to others.

Campers and caravanners are also well provided for by the convenient camping ground so beautifully sited beside the shores of Loch Morlich, with its golden sandy beaches in the shadow of the snow-wreathed Cairngorms. Ramblers and mountain climbers have ample facilities for exploring the high peaks, and there is provision for such sports as bathing, boating and fishing, as well as

SCHOOLBOYS FROM GLASGOW DESCENDING THE BRAES TO
RYVOAN PASS AND THE GREEN LOCHAN

for expeditions on foot or on ski over the icy peaks in winter.
Recently a fine new road has been built from Coylumbridge to
Loch Morlich and the ski-ing slopes, and a chair lift and ski tows
have been added. The new Loch Morlich Youth Hostel will be an
invaluable help to the many young people who come to the Park
on foot, often from far afield.

In return for these privileges of free access to the hills, visitors are
expected to observe those rules of good conduct designed to protect
the safety and amenity of the nation's property, and of the whole
countryside. In particular, they are asked to avoid leaving litter,
lighting fires, or damaging fences, and to respect the haunts of the
region's unique wild life, both plant and animal.

Now that Speyside has rightly become a place of pilgrimage for
all who love the wild beauty of our moors and mountains, I am
glad to say—speaking if I may for all who live in the district as well
as for myself—that we shall do all we can to make welcome the ever-
increasing numbers of people, young and old, who will share our
lovely country with us.

CONTENTS

ACKNOWLEDGMENTS

THE VERSES that appear at the heads of the chapters are, with one exception, taken from the poem *Rothiemurchus*, by the late William Jeffrey, published in his *Sea Glimmer* (Maclellan, Glasgow, 1948, 6s.,) and are included by kind permission of Mrs. Jeffrey and the publishers.

THE COVER DESIGN was drawn by Mr. C. T. McKenna.

THE HEADPIECE DRAWINGS are the work of Miss Vivien Hislop, D.A.

THE PHOTOGRAPHS. Thanks are due to the following photographers who have so ably depicted the Forest Park and its surroundings under the varying moods of the seasons and the weather, as well as some of its most charming denizens:

Messrs. Aberdeen Journals, Ltd., for the picture on page 12; Mr. R. M. Adam for the frontispiece and the views on pages 10, 15, 21, 22, 23, 45, 96; Lord Malcolm Douglas Hamilton for those on pages 59, 61, 62, 63, 74; the Assistant Director of H.M. Geological Survey, Edinburgh, for those on pages 16, 17; Mr. Seton Gordon, for the bird studies on pages 30, 31, 32, 33; Mr. A. C. Gray for the view on page 70; Mr. John Markham for those on pages 47, 71 106, 112; Mr. W. A. Poucher for those on pages 6, 24, 27, 43; Mr. W. S. Thomson for those on pages 73, 104; Mr. T. MacKenzie for that on page 64; Mr. B. H. Humble for the photos on pages ii, iv, 11, 19, 51, 56, 70, 103; Mr. Charles Cromar for that on page 97; and Mr. F. A. Bartlet for that on page 53; *The Scotsman* for that on page 111; Mr. L. S. Paterson for that on page 68; Tom Weir for that on page 1; Mr. M. N. P. Utsi for those on pages 37, 40; Murray G. Scott for that on page 80; the British Travel and Holidays Association for that on page 3; and Messrs. Valentines of Dundee for those on pages 84 and 89.

THE MAPS are based on the Ordnance Survey, by permission of the Director General.

THE BIBLIOGRAPHY has been contributed by Miss M. O MacDougall, Burgh Librarian, Inverness.

First published	..	*May, 1949*
Fourth Edition	..	*January, 1966*

LOCH MORLICH AND THE MONADH LIATH FROM CAIRNGORM
A glacial moraine, now undergoing erosion, occupies the foreground.

Let the eye at this living instant survey from a vantage point
The swelling majesty of our mountains and their infolded peace,
And take in the rich greenery and warm heath of the forest
And note how, holding time in suspense,
They absorb all sound into silence, all movement into the trance of stone.

INTRODUCTION

By PROFESSOR JOHN WALTON

The establishment of a Forest Park in 1948 by the Forestry
Commission at the Queen's Forest of Glen More extended the parts
of Scotland to which the public has access and in which the country
lover, climber and naturalist can wander in complete freedom.
This freedom, however, carries with it a responsibility to preserve
the beauty and natural treasures of the area, and to guard against
doing anything which will spoil it for others. The Cairngorms, and
particularly the Glen More part of them, are representative of

what is most impressive in the Eastern Highlands. The great precipices and corries round the edge of the summit plateaux, flanked by the massive slopes of the mountainside, seem to form a gigantic fortress standing firm against the onslaught of the elements. The great granite masses seem rooted and unshakable.

In contrast to this grim splendour of the mountains we have all the beauty of the living world, the alpine and arctic types of flowers, the pinewoods, and, in the centre, that clear and sparkling sheet of water, Loch Morlich.

FEATURES OF INTEREST NEAR THE PARK

LOCH AN EILEIN, 6 miles from Glen More Lodge by a driving road running due south from Coylumbridge, deserves a visit for its romantic setting amidst ancient pinewoods that have happily escaped the ravages of the wars. The ruined castle on its islet was founded about the fifteenth century, and extended four times thereafter. It was held by the Mackintoshes before 1539, by the Gordons until 1567, and has since remained in the possession of the Grants.

The hill of CRAIGELLACHIE (1,700 feet), commemorated by the Grants' war cry of "Stand fast, Craigellachie!" is well worth ascending for the fine views it commands both up and down Strath Spey, and across to the Cairngorms.

Also within reach of the Park are some of the most remote and beautiful of the Highland straths and glens, particularly those of the Findhorn (Strath Dearn), the Dulnain, the Feshie, and the Tromie. Loch Alvie, Loch Insch, Loch Garten and Loch Pityoulish all lie within a few miles of the Park, and their beautiful tree-clad shores well merit a visit.

The Glen More Forest Park is complementary to the Argyll and the Queen Elizabeth Forest Parks, for the latter are typical of the Western Highlands region, where the mountains are more irregular in form and where the ash and oak woods in the straths take the place of the pine woods.

On the 9th July, 1954, a large area lying to the south and southwest of the Forest Park (see map on rear end paper) was declared a nature reserve under the management of the Nature Conservancy, 12 Hope Terrace, Edinburgh, 9. This reserve, the Cairngorms Nature Reserve, is now the largest in Britain and includes nearly 64 square miles of mountain and forest. The aim of the Nature Conservancy is to preserve the native flora and fauna, but the walking and climbing public, provided they observe the Country Code of good conduct, are welcome within the Reserve, and only under exceptional circumstances will they be requested to avoid for a few weeks in the year certain restricted areas where birds or animals are breeding. The collection of specimens is not allowed without special permission from the Nature Conservancy, and then only for scientific purposes.

This large area now comprising both Forest Park and the Cairngorms Nature Reserve, on which plant and animal life is protected, will undoubtedly help to keep in a vigorous state the wild life in this important and representative part of the Cairngorms, and provide scope for the study of our native plants and animals living in natural conditions. It provides a great variety of habitats ranging from the exposed wind-swept summits with their late-lying snow, to the moorlands and forests at lower altitudes.

Grateful acknowledgment is here made to those who have so willingly co-operated in the production of this Guide, the writers of the chapters dealing with the various aspects of the Park, its inhabitants and its history, the artists whose work adorns its pages, the photographers to whose skill and artistic judgment we owe the fine illustrations, and the local staff of the Forestry Commission, whose detailed knowledge of the district has proved invaluable.

My special thanks are due to the Publications Officer of the Forestry Commission, Mr. H. L. Edlin, whose effective assistance has made the production of this book a pleasant task. The greater part of any success this booklet achieves must be credited to him.

THE CAMPING GROUND

ROBIN OG AND THE FAIRY PUFF BALL

HISTORY AND TRADITION

By A. Macpherson Grant

For centuries the Privy Council of Scotland maintained the Highlands in a state of submission, keeping them in subjection by repressive measures. Glen More, however, does not appear in their records; either the district was too well-behaved for censure, or else there were no inhabitants. This last is the obvious choice; Glen More meant trees and little else.

But though one cannot refer to clan battles and local traditions in Glen More itself, there is ample history all around it. To the north lay Clan Grant and nearby is Rothiemurchus—home of Grants and Shaws; to the south is Badenoch, crossed and recrossed by forces loyal or revolutionary; to the west was the country of the Clan Chattan, an uneasy confederation of Mackintoshes, Macphersons, MacGillivrays, and a dozen other septs.

The Earls of Huntly, to whom the Government of the district was entrusted by the Crown, divided the land on terms to the local chiefs, who kept a large number of restless adherents on an insufficient acreage of soil. Nominally, these adherents were supposed to uphold the banner of their overlord; in practice they obeyed their chief. It

4

was a system within a system, and feudal in name only. In 1684 the fourth Marquis of Huntly was created Duke of Gordon, and his family continued to own great tracts of land in Strath Spey. At one time their domains extended from sea to sea, from Speymouth to Fort William. Their most important stronghold was the castle of Ruthven near Kingussie, and it is only worthy of such a historical spot that the main road close by should be persistently haunted at night.

Strath Spey is a valley of music, romance, and tradition, but always martial, as witness the annals of the 51st Highland Division. Badenoch was forever the scene of restlessness. Montrose traversed it many times on his unbelievable marches, and in the '45 Prince Charlie's forces, coming from Glenfinnan, consolidated themselves there and enrolled Cluny Macpherson, a local hero, who hid himself for nine years among his native hills, while the royal forces searched for him in vain. Hundreds of people could have located him, but in spite of a princely bribe, none did so. Badenoch prides itself on its nobility to this day.

A still more extraordinary story is that of Mackintosh, chief of his clan, who served through the '45 in the Hanoverian forces, while his wife, young Lady Anne, raised the clan on behalf of Prince Charlie. Mackintosh did not forfeit his estate, and Lady Anne was not hanged, but one wonders how this domestic difference was settled in later years.

Scarcely any of the leading men in Lower Badenoch joined the Jacobite Risings. They remained neutral and in 1715 actually imprisoned in Loch an Eilein Castle one of their number suspected of a desire to join the Hanoverians.

One cannot be long in the district before hearing of Jean, Duchess of Gordon. She raised many recruits for the Gordon Highlanders, but the story that she rode about holding a guinea between her lips and allowing recruits to take hold of it similarly is untrue. She is buried at Kinrara, in the wood near the house, and her grave belongs to the Gordon Highlanders.

Glen More continued in the ownership of the Dukes of Gordon until its acquisition by the Forestry Commissioners in 1923. Let us turn from the study of its past and have a day amongst its trees. Be an animal for the day, and associate yourself with the local animals who really own the place. Let these animals be: it's their country, not yours. Look how a dainty roebuck springs into view and how madam will deceive you as to the whereabouts of her fawn, among the bracken. That rare little bird is the crested tit—but do spare its nest—nor seek the home of the handsome peregrine. Talk

5

THE OLD TRACK THROUGH THE PATH OF RYVOAN

of it, and a crowd of people may come out with guns. If you are so lucky as to find that most beautiful and rarest of Highland woodland plants, the *Linnaea borealis,* forget where the plant is, or a platoon of spade-men may come and dig it up.

Going further afield, there are historic sites to be visited in the island castle of Loch an Eilein, the churchyard of Insch beyond Kincraig, and the battlefield of Culloden, which last is easily reached by road from Aviemore. The remains of prehistoric peoples persist in the Picts House just east of Kingussie, and in the stone circles around Aviemore village.

The hills bounding Glen More, nowadays called the Cairngorms or Blue Hills, were formerly known as the Monadh Ruadh (Red-brown Hills) to distinguish them from the hills across the Spey still called the Monadh Liath, or Grey Hills. These don't afford much scenery but offer hill tracks towards Inverness.

There are ruins of shielings in plenty among the Monadh Liath, and here a word as to a shieling. About May every year the women and children were escorted to their temporary shieling homes and there left by the men to their summer task of rearing young animals and butter-making till summer was over. The Highland boys learnt their agility tending young cattle amongst the hills, and were kept occupied unwillingly, in the evening, by learning to knit. *Ruidh* and *airidh* were the common names for shielings.

The loneliness of the women's work found expression in the

6

many touching shieling songs which are the most beautiful in Gaelic poetry. Here is the translation of a passage from one such song:

> "But 'tis pity that I and my sweetheart of flowing locks were not in the little green clump, where the wood pigeon will crow; in the rushy thicket in which would be the roebuck—and the heather around us in dark green folds."

GHOSTS AND FAIRIES

The Cairngorms are traditionally the home of that strange mythical creature known in Gaelic as the *famh* (pronounced "fav", and normally signifying a mole). According to the *Statistical Account of Scotland*, Kirkmichael parish (1794), "In summer mornings it issues from its lurking places, emitting a kind of glutinous matter fatal to horses if they happen to eat the grass upon which it has been deposited. It is somewhat larger than a mole, of a brownish colour, with a large head disproportionate to its body. Other quadrupeds once indigenous to the Grampian Mountains are now extinct, such as the *torc neimh* of wild boar."

James Hogg mentions the "fahm" in his poem *The Queen's Wake*, and the anonymous editor of Chambers's 1841 edition of that work provides the following information:

"Fahm is a little ugly monster, who frequents the summits of the mountains around Glen Avin, and no other place in the world that I know of. My guide, D. M'Queen, declared that he had himself seen him, and, by his description, Fahm appears to be no native of this world, but an occasional visitant, whose intentions are evil and dangerous. He is only seen about the break of day, and on the highest verge of the mountain. His head is twice as large as his whole body beside; and if any living creature cross the track over which he has passed, before the sun shine upon it, certain death is the consequence."

It is possible that this curious legend arose from the survival into early historic times of some small arctic beast (such as the lemming) that has since become extinct in Scotland.

A more recent discovery is the *Fear Liath Mòr* or Great Grey Man, said by certain modern climbers to haunt the summit of Ben Macdhui. He is a ghostly figure who follows one with pattering feet. Snow whirls can look surprisingly human at times, and eerie is the sough of the wind in the corrie!

Fairies are said to dance on moonlight nights around the peculiar little conical hill just above Lochan Uaine. Once a wandering shepherd named Robin Og stole their tiny fairy bagpipes, but when dawn came he found himself holding nothing except a puff ball to which a few blades of grass were attached!

7

AT THE CEILIDH

THE OLD WAYS OF LIFE
IN STRATH SPEY

By MISS I. F. GRANT

In a sparsely occupied country like the Highlands abundant vestiges
may be traced of the people who once lived there, although the
appearance of Strath Spey has been altered to some extent by the
clearance of some forests and the establishment of others, and there
have been similar changes in the location of agricultural land. In
the old days the floors of the straths were largely swamps, only useful
for cutting the coarse natural grass to serve as winter feeding. Some
of this land is once more uncultivated, but old ditches and embank-
ments are reminders of more prosperous days for farming. Of such
good times the Napoleonic wars formed a highwater-mark.

Means of communication seldom followed the valleys. The old
drove roads, mere tracks, generally crossed them and went over the
hills. Several can still be traced on the Cairngorms and the Monadh
Liath. Raiding clansmen, adventurous packmen, the great droves of
cattle that were the Highlanders' main source of wealth and were
yearly driven down to the Southern markets, all used them. Two
such roads actually cross the Forest Park, one linking Aviemore

8

with Strath Nethy by the Ryvoan Pass, the other—the famous "Caterans Road"—running from Ryvoan south-westwards along the lower slopes of Cairn Gorm towards Upper Badenoch.

The layout of Highland farms varied according to the configuration of the land, but in the wider straths the townships were generally grouped along the hill slopes (the Gaelic *baile*, township, survives in many place-names beginning with "Bal"). Eight joint-tenants was a convenient number, for each tenant provided a beast, horse or ox, for the team that drew the clumsy wooden plough that tilled all the lands of the township. Regular fields or fences there were none. Patches of the best, and most rock-free land, called the "in-field", received all the manure and were kept under constant crops of rye and inferior oats and barley. A proportion of the less suitable land, the "outfield", was cropped in the same way till it was exhausted and then was abandoned for a time. Turnips were not grown and there was no sown hay, so the animals fared badly in the winter. But in the summer the beasts and the people who looked after them had a very happy time, for they went up to the shielings in the sweet hill pastures.

Often still one comes across traces of the old cultivation, patches of narrow, crooked ridges, often on very steep slopes. The old methods gave a very poor return. When the seasons were unfavourable most people went short of food for part of the year. Work was very laborious; corn was threshed with the flail and reaped with the sickle. The new system of separate holdings and regular fields tilled under a rotation of crops, was developed in southern Scotland in the eighteenth century and thence gradually made its way into the Highlands. The making of field drains, which brought much of our best land into cultivation, came later, and tile drainage was only being introduced about a hundred years ago.

In the old days everyone grew a "spot" of flax—often in the large gardens of which one sees traces near old cottages. The people themselves performed the rather unpleasant processes required for preparing the lint, and the women of the household spun the yarn for clothing and household napery, and it was woven by the local weaver. Wool was dyed and spun at home and woven by the weaver into cloth and plaids and blankets. Harness (mostly of wood), baskets and wooden bowls and platters were made at home from local materials. Such things as milk cogs and cruisie lamps were made by the village cooper and blacksmith. The neighbours would unite in building each others' houses, small but warm, and easily added to or repaired because all the materials were found to hand. The tinkers made horn spoons or would hammer a coin into a brooch.

LOOKING DOWN RYVOAN PASS TO THE GREEN LOCHAN
The far snow-wreathed hollow is Coire an Lochain, the notch in the hills marks
Creag a' Chalamain.

The people's pleasures were also home made. Mrs. Grant of
Laggan, writing of the upper valley of the Spey, said that in every
cottage there was a musician and in every hamlet a poet. Gathered
about the glowing peatfire to spin and carry on their other crafts, the
people not only sang old songs and told old tales, but they impro-
vised, wittily if not always charitably. Their great collection of
oral traditions about their legendary heroes, the Feine, was con-
stantly being added to, like a serial story. It was at Ruthven, just up
the strath, that James Macpherson, the young schoolmaster, learnt
the stories on which he based his *Ossian*, which entranced the
literary world of the eighteenth century.

It is a strange thing that the work rhythms of these long-dead
Highlanders should still survive when so much else has vanished, but
our loveliest traditional song-tunes were made to help people through
the drudgery of working with the simplest tools. The people lived in
an atmosphere of song and their lilt is with us yet.

Anyone who would like to see examples of the old implements and plenishings, of the lovely fabrics and of the other crafts, and how the houses were built and furnished, can visit the most comprehensive collection of its kind in Scotland, *Am Fasgadh*, the Highland Folk Museum at Kingussie, which is open to the public in June, July, August and September. This museum, first established by Dr. I. F. Grant in 1934, has been acquired by the four Scottish universities of Aberdeen, Edinburgh, Glasgow and St. Andrews. Their aim is to make it a centre which will not only remind Scotland and her visitors of the origins of materials and customs, but which will become a show place to world students of Highland folklore and antiquities.

There is also a fine collection of Highland antiquities in the Burgh Museum, Inverness.

SAILING ON LOCH MORLICH

Space of an amplitude gigantic fashioned our mountains and forest,
Moulding carries in the gray crags for the knuckles of the wind,
Spreading slopes of heather and the bristling pine . . .

GEOLOGY

By PROFESSOR J. G. C. ANDERSON

The Cairngorm Mountains, which include four of the five highest
peaks in the British Isles, and by far the most extensive area over
3,000 feet, form a distinctive part of the Scottish Highlands. Their
individuality is largely a reflection of their geological character,
for the main part of the range has been sculptured from one of the
largest granite masses in the country, with a total outcrop of some
160 square miles.

It is the prevalence of the granite which gave rise to the old name
of the mountains, the Monadh Ruadh or Red Hills—in contrast to
the Monadh Liath or Grey Hills on the opposite side of the Spey,
which are composed mainly of schist. On the other hand the modern

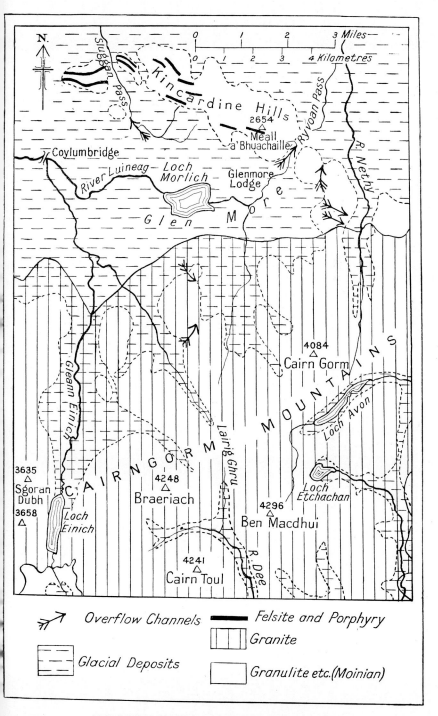

GEOLOGICAL SKETCH MAP OF THE FOREST PARK

name has passed into mineralogical terminology through being applied to the well-known ornamental stone—a variety of quartz.

Though the Cairngorm granite is of great antiquity—it was formed by the consolidation of molten material in late Silurian or early Devonian times some 300 million years ago—it is by no means the oldest rock of the district, as it was intruded into still more ancient metamorphic rocks, mainly granulites (or psammitic schists as they are sometimes called). The granulites were formed by the metamorphism, or alteration by intense heat and pressure, of sandstones. Interbedded with the granulites are thin layers of mica-schist (sometimes called pelitic schist) produced by the alteration of originally clayey sediments. Igneous rocks other than the granite which occur in the district include irregular veins of pegmatite and sheet-like intrusions of felsite and porphyry.

Throughout most of the lower ground the "solid" rocks mentioned above are hidden under a mantle of unconsolidated superficial or drift deposits, nearly all of which are of glacial origin. The glacial deposits are particularly thick and widespread along the northern side of the Cairngorm Mountains, where their presence has encouraged the growth of the great Rothiemurchus Forest.

THE METAMORPHIC ROCKS

The metamorphic rocks are often spoken of as the Central Highland Granulites, and are grey or pinkish, fine- to medium-grained rocks composed essentially of the minerals quartz and felspar, with scattered flakes of mica. Thin layers, very rich in mica, are present at irregular intervals. Weathering along these gives the granulites a characteristically flaggy appearance.

The Central Highland Granulites form part of the Moinian Assemblage, a major sub-division of the Highland metamorphic strata. Their age is a matter of dispute, but they are almost certainly pre-Cambrian, that is, older than the earliest formation with recognisable fossils.

The granulites, along with other Highland strata, were involved in Silurian times in major horizontal movements of the earth's crust accompanying what is known as the Caledonian Period of mountain building, which brought into existence a great chain, with a general north-easterly trend, in Scotland and Scandinavia. To appreciate the major structures resulting from these disturbances requires the study of a wide area, but the minor effects are seen in the small-scale folding and distortion of the metamorphic strata visible in numerous rock-faces in the district.

THE GRAND OLD NATURAL PINE FOREST OF CREAGAN GORM
The far hills are Cairn Lochan and (right) Creag an Leth-Choin—the Lurcher's Crag.

PEGMATITE VEINS

Throughout much of the area the granulites are penetrated by thin irregular veins termed pegmatites. These are of the same composition as granite, that is to say they consist of the minerals quartz, felspar and mica, but are much more coarsely crystalline. Most of the pegmatites are earlier than, and unconnected with, the main Cairngorm granite.

THE CAIRNGORM GRANITE

The granite is normally a fairly coarse-grained rock composed of quartz and red felspar with a little mica. Fine-grained varieties also occur in some areas. The granite is usually cut by widely spaced, strongly marked, rectangular joints, weathering along which gives rise to the "mural" or walled appearance characteristic of the precipitous sides of the great corries in the heart of the range.

15

THE LOCHAN IN THE COIRE AN LOCHAIN
A moraine-dammed lochan.

It is in veins and cavities in the granite that the "cairngorms" occur. The "cairngorm" crystals, which are generally associated with felspar and mica, vary in colour from yellow to black; they are often somewhat smoky. "Cairngorms" are also found as loose crystals in the disintegrated granite debris which covers much of the Cairngorm Plateau, and they occur as pebbles in some of the rivers. The search for "cairngorms" was at one time a profitable industry, but it has been discontinued for many years owing to the import of cheap foreign stones. Beryls are not infrequent in some localities and are know locally as "green cairngorms".

FELSITES AND PORPHYRIES

At some localities in the northern part of the area, thin, sheet-like bodies of igneous rock (technically termed sills) may be seen in the granulites. These are of a pinkish colour and are of the same composition as the granite but much finer in grain. The felsites are even-grained: the porphyries contain scattered large crystals set in a fine-grained matrix.

TOPOGRAPHY

The striking relief of the district is not, as often imagined, the direct result either of the earth movements already mentioned or of the intrusion of the granite. The scenery, as is the case throughout

16

THE GLACIAL OVERFLOW CHANNEL BELOW CREAG A' CHALAMAIN

the Highlands, is the result of sculpture. The Cairngorm Mountains are portions of a high plateau deeply dissected by river valleys.

The slope of the primitive Highland plateau as a whole was south-easterly and the original rivers followed this direction. The Lairig Ghru is a relic of one of these "consequent" valleys, as they are termed. As time went on so the "consequent" valleys were inter-sected by north-easterly flowing "subsequent" rivers, following the old north-easterly "grain" of the country, of which the Spey is a notable example.

The evolution of the broad topographic features was complete before the glacial epoch, but erosion by ice was responsible for modifications such as the formation of corries and of broad U-shaped valleys. Many minor details of the landscape, too, are due either to glacial action or to the presence of glacial deposits.

GLACIATION

The glacial history of the region is complex, and in the present account it is possible to indicate only its salient features. At one time it is probable that the whole of the Cairngorms was covered by a great ice-sheet. As far as the district around Loch Morlich is con-cerned, however, chief interest attaches to a later stage during which the higher Cairngorms were mostly free from ice, while Glen More was occupied by a great lobe of ice branching off a major glacier coming down the Spey valley. The Glen More glacier, as it may be termed, was responsible for the deposition of most, if not all, of the glacial deposits of the district. Proof of this statement lies in the fact that the majority of the stones in these glacial deposits consist of various types of schist; if ice from the Cairngorms had been responsible, granite should have predominated.

The glacial deposits are of various types. Lateral moraines deposited along the margins of the Glen More glacier form an almost continuous series of low ridges, for the most part at between the 1,500 and the 2,000 feet levels, along the northern slopes of the Cairngorms and the southern slopes of the Kincardine Hills. Ground moraine, formed under the ice, is represented by the comparatively smooth sheet of clayey drift which covers the southern slope of the Kincardine Hills.

By far the most widespread glacial deposits of the district, however, are the gravelly morainic deposits which floor most of the low ground. These have a typical moundy or hummocky form and consist of a rather ill-assorted mixture of sand, gravel and clay. They were deposited at the ice front during various stages of retreat of the ice.

At its maximum the Glen More ice escaped northwards through the Ryvoan Pass. Successive pauses in its retreat southwards through the pass are indicated by the moraines which cross the glen at intervals. Above each of these lies a peaty flat marking the site of a small tarn held up for a time by the moraine below. The green waters of An Lochan Uaine still occupy the highest of these ponded lochans.

Loch Morlich itself is a large "kettle-hole", a hollow left on the final melting of a great block of ice—possibly a last remnant of the stagnant Glen More glacier. Other deposits, differing in character from moraines and termed "fluvioglacial", form very extensive terraces in Gleann Einich and smaller terraces at the northern entrance to the Lairig Ghru. They were deposited by running water in temporary lochs brought into being when tongues of the Glen More glacier dammed the valleys in which they lie.

The blockage of the normal drainage by the ice also had the effect of diverting the water through various overflow channels which on the disappearance of the ice were left as dry valleys or gullies. Several of these overflow channels, for instance, breach the ridge of Stac na h'Iolaire east of Glen More Lodge, and were formed when ice forced the water draining from the northern slopes of Cairn Gorm to escape eastwards into Strath Nethy. Another forms a conspicuous notch in the ridge of Creag a' Chalamain, on the east side of the stream draining northwards from the Lairig Ghru.

At one stage, too, the Sluggan pass functioned as an overflow channel. (See sketch map on page 13.)

POST-GLACIAL DEPOSITS

The alluvial terraces along the course of many of the streams, and the peat covering parts of the flatter ground, are examples of deposits formed after the disappearance of the ice. Comparatively recent deposits which contribute to the beauty of the district are the sandy beaches of Loch Morlich and the sand dunes at its eastern end.

BIBLIOGRAPHY

The geology of the National Forest Park area is shown on sheet 74 of the 1-inch to the mile Geological Map of Scotland; the Cairngorm Mountains as a whole are shown on sheets 64, 65, 74 and 75.

Geological Survey Memoirs dealing with parts of the Cairngorm Mountains are:

BARROW, G. and others. 1912. The Geology of the Districts of Braemar, Ballater and Glen Clova. (Explanation of Sheet 65.)

BARROW, G. and others. 1913. The Geology of Upper Strathspey, Gaick and the Forest of Atholl. (Explanation of Sheet 64.)

HINXMAN, L. W. 1896. West Aberdeenshire, Banffshire, Parts of Elgin and Inverness. (Explanation of Sheet 75.)

HINXMAN, L. W. and others. 1915. The Geology of Mid-Strathspey and Strathdearn. (Explanation of Sheet 74.)

READ, H. H. and A. G. MACGREGOR. 1948. British Regional Geology: The Grampian Highlands (2nd Edition.)

SETTING OUT FOR THE SUMMITS

But mostly to the visiting eye of contemplation
A rich harvest may be gleaned from our forest—
Pines of strength, armoured with the antiquity of eagles,
Roarers in the storm, and in the calms
The abode of golden-plumaged and responsive peace;

THE VEGETATION
OF THE PARK

By Professor John Walton

To those who take an interest in wild plants the Glen More Forest Park offers an almost inexhaustible supply of subjects for study and delight. Here they will find a magnificent display of mountain vegetation ranging from the pine forests to the arctic-alpine flora of the summits. Large areas of the mountain-sides bear an abundance of plants which occur in only relatively small and scattered patches on other British mountains. Compared with some other Scottish mountains, there are perhaps fewer of the specially rare alpine species. This is no doubt due to differences in climate and chemical composition of the rocks.

Mountain plants have always had a special attraction for those interested in botanical matters. This is in part due to the fact that many of them are found in relatively inaccessible places and then only after considerable bodily exertion. An arduous climb may be amply rewarded by such unforgettable visions as cushions of moss

STARRY SAXIFRAGE, SAXIFRAGA STELLARIS

campion (*Silene acaulis*) covered with its brilliant pink blossoms contrasting gloriously with the inhospitable stony places in which it grows at high altitudes, or of the starry saxifrage (*Saxifraga stellaris*). The plants which grow on the exposed hill slopes and at high altitudes appear dwarfed or stunted, but in contrast to this many of them when they flower do so very profusely and may make a most conspicuous display. Several species which are found at these high altitudes are relics of the arctic flora which existed in Britain during the Ice Age, and a flora with many of the same species is found in countries of the far North, e.g., Northern Canada, Greenland, Spitsbergen, and Novaya Zemlya. In these countries we find the moss campion and dwarf willow abundant at sea level. We suppose that when the Ice Age passed away and lower-lying areas acquired a temperate climate, these arctic plants which were inhabitants of the lower-lying ice-free areas, persisted on the higher summits where the conditions most nearly approximate to those found in the Arctic today, and where they had not to compete with plants suited to warmer conditions.

The Glen More Forest Park includes the northern slopes and corries of the Cairn Gorm, Cairn Lochan and Creag an Leth-choin ridge, the strath drained by the Luineag river and the southern slopes of the ridge of mountains (the Kincardine Hills) that runs north-west from the Ryvoan Pass to the Sluggan Pass. Practically the whole of this area is over 1,000 feet above sea level, but owing to the shelter provided by the mountains the limit of tree growth is

MOSS CAMPION, SILENE ACAULIS

considerably higher than in most parts of Scotland. Indeed the plantations extend to over 1,500 feet and scattered groups of trees may be found at even higher altitudes. The forest and plantations are mainly situated on areas which have a covering of glacial deposits which provide a deep enough hold for the tree roots. In a few level places on the slope at about 2,000 feet, there are small accumulations of peat in which there may be seen buried stumps of pine, clear evidence that at one time the forests extended to a considerably greater altitude up the mountain sides than they do today. Relics of forests now buried in the peat are found in several parts of Scotland where no forests exist today. The most extensive is on the Moor of Rannoch, where exposed tree stumps may be seen where the main road runs through cuttings in the peat moor.

DWARF CORNEL, CHAMAEPERICLYMENUM SUECIUM

This eastern part of the Scottish Highlands has a smaller annual rainfall than the westerly part: probably less than two-thirds of that to which the Argyll Forest Park is subject. It is also colder in the winter. The main mass of the Cairngorms consist of granites and felsite while the West Highlands including the Argyll Park consist principally of schists and gneisses.

These differences in climate and geological composition determine very largely the differences we observe between the floras and vegetation of the two regions. In the Argyll Park there are large areas of wet, boggy moorland on peat whereas in the Glen More Park the drier conditions favour a greater proportion of heathland. There is, on account of the greater general altitude and smaller rainfall, less luxuriant growth of mosses and liverworts in the Glen

CAIRN GORM AND THE THREE NORTH-FACING CORRIES
Coire Cas, Coire an t-Sneachda, and Coire an Lochain

More Park than in the Argyll Park.

The vegetation of the park may be divided into several regions: the aquatic and semi-aquatic vegetation of the loch and its shore, the meadowland, the forests, the open hillsides, moorland, the corries, and the vegetation of the summits.

Loch Morlich, which lies in the centre of the park, is shallow and is not more than about 25 feet deep at its deepest part. At the east end of the loch there is a sandy beach which is practically bare of vegetation except for a few pines and some tussocks of marram grass, here at its maximum height above sea level in Britain. The prevalent west wind blows up the loch and the sandy beach has been formed by wind and wave action. The northern shore shelves very gently and there is a stretch of stones and small boulders which is covered by the loch waters after heavy rainfall. The western end of the loch tends to be muddy. There are few submerged aquatic plants; the water lobelia may be seen with its pale blue-flowered inflorescence projecting above the surface of the water. On all stony shores we find the shore weed (*Littorella uniflora*), the lesser spearwort, *Lycopodium inundatum* and *Hammarbya paludosa*. Alders, willows and pines are found growing on or close to the shore and along the banks of the burn; at least two species of bladderwort (*Utricularia*) are to be found in the muddy shallows at the west end of the loch.

The meadowland extends from the head of the loch eastwards to the lower slopes of Mam Suim. It is a lush grassland with sedges and rushes in the moister areas. Parts of it have been cultivated and used for pasture.

The slightly higher better-drained ground bears forest. There are still considerable areas in the Park in an almost natural state, with wide spaces between the trees which are of different sizes and ages; here we find a rich ground flora of small shrubby plants. The Scots pine (*Pinus sylvestris*) is the principal native tree and is the dominant woodland tree in this region. Some botanists regard the form found in this area as a distinct variety. It differs in some respects from the types of Scots pine found elsewhere in Britain. There is little doubt that pine forest has persisted here ever since the close of the Ice Age. Birches and occasional junipers occur among the pines and with them we find heather or ling (*Calluna vulgaris*), blaeberry (*Vaccinium myrtillus*) and cowberry (*Vaccinium vitis-idaea*) all of which are in the form of small shrubs. We occasionally come across serrate winter-green (*Pyrola media*), *Moneses uniflora*, chickweed-wintergreen (*Trientalis*), and *Linnaea borealis*.

On the slopes of the mountains where there are no woodlands or plantations, and in the small glens, there are occasional trees of pine, birch and rowan, and bushes of juniper and cowberry are abundant, but blaeberry, bell heather (*Erica cinerea*), bearberry (*Arctostaphylos*) and the petty whin (*Genista anglica*) also occur. In the shelter provided by these larger plants we may find the lesser twayblade (*Listera cordata*) and in the more sheltered places on peaty soil the cloudberry (*Rubus chamaemorus*). Where the surface is wind-swept, bearberry, crowberry (*Empetrum nigrum*), and stunted plants of ling and bell heather are predominant, with occasionally *Lycopodium alpinum* and cat's ear (*Antennaria dioica*).

Several of these plants produce edible berries which may provide welcome refreshment on a hot summer day. The best is the blaeberry (bilberry or whortleberry), which is particularly abundant in the open woodland along the sides of the Allt Mor burn by the path from the Glen More Lodge to Cairn Gorm. The berries are bluish black with a distinct bloom. The crowberry (*Empetrum*) has almost black shiny berries which are rather tasteless, but the juice they provide is refreshing. When cooked they produce a deep purple

3   25

juice. The cowberry with bright red berries (*Vaccinium vitis-idaea*), sometimes called the Scots cranberry, makes excellent cranberry jam but is not palatable raw. The cloudberry (*Rubus chamaemorus*) has fruits of a pale peach colour when ripe. These are very good eating, but they are not present in any considerable quantity in the Park.

In wet boggy areas along the sides of the burns there are the cross-leaved heath (*Erica tetralix*), bog asphodel, spotted orchis, butterwort and sundew.

Between 2,500 feet and 3,000 feet above sea level the slopes are drier and stony and have no continuous covering of vegetation. The plants are all stunted or lie very close to the ground. Here we find little prostrate shrubs of *Loiseleuria procumbens*, a close relative of our cultivated azaleas. It has small evergreen leaves like a heath and the plants may be covered with very small rose-coloured flowers in late spring. Along with it we may find cushions of moss campion with their bright pink flowers, *Lycopodium selago*, and the very small rush *Juncus trifidus*. In sheltered depressions there may be alpine lady's mantle (*Alchemilla alpina*), bog vaccinium (*V. uliginosum*) and dwarf cornel (*Chamaepericlymenum suecium*), which has four large petal-like bracts surrounding a group of very small dark-coloured flowers producing a bunch of scarlet berries in the late summer. Lichens and small mosses are abundant.

Above 3,000 feet the vegetation becomes sparser with occasional low cushions of moss campion, the rush *Juncus trifidus*, crowberry and the dwarf or least willow (*Salix herbacea*). The latter although a true willow would hardly be recognized as such by the uninitiated, for its twigs rise but an inch or two from the ground. In August when the catkins are in fruit, the hairy seeds which they release make the plant look as if someone had spread a thin layer of cotton wool over it. In the corries where shelter is greater, there is an admixture of plants which occur elsewhere at lower altitudes, with those which are found high up. For example the globe-flower (*Trollius*) occurs in wet regions on stream banks in the bottoms of the corries, but it is also found elsewhere in Scotland as a plant of wet meadowland.

We find occasional specimens of *Saussurea alpina* and Scotch asphodel (*Tofieldia pusilla*). On the rock ledges are various species of saxifrage, *Polygonum viviparum* and many mosses and liverworts peculiar to high altitudes.

In a few places above 3,000 feet snow may lie all the year round, and on the ground which is covered with snow late on into the early summer we find a characteristic assemblage of small plants such as *Gnaphalium supinum*, with mosses and liverworts.

This beautiful and interesting stretch of the Scottish Highlands is now open to the public in greater numbers than ever. In the winter

26

MEALL A' BHUACHAILLE FROM LOCH MORLICH

when the ground is under snow the plants are safe, but in the summer the chair lifts will bring many more visitors. It is to be hoped that all who visit it will do all they can to help in preserving its natural treasures. In particular visitors should not pick flowers which they discover and above all should not remove any plants. Many of the specially interesting and characteristic mountain plants are just managing to hold their own, and no more, in the struggle for existence, and if man's interference is put in the balance against them they will soon become extinct in the Park.

BIBLIOGRAPHY

The Ecology of the Cairngorms:
  Part I. The environment and the altitudinal zonation of the Vegetation. Watt, A. S. and Jones, E. W. 1948. *Journ. of Ecology*, vol. 36, pp. 283-304.
  Part II. The Mountain Callunetum. Metcalfe, G. 1950. *Journ. of Ecology*, vol. 38, pp. 46-74.
  Part III. The Empetrum-Vaccinium Zone. Burges, A. 1951. *Journ. of Ecology*, vol. 39, pp. 271-284.
General:
  The British Islands and their Vegetation. Sir Arthur Tansley. Cambridge, 1939.

The hearth and ploughs of men touch but the fringe of our forest,
The seamew follows no furrow in its midst.
There the curlew and the snipe ply their lonely orchestrations,
The grouse and the raven dwell,
And the eagle from his planetary gyre sinks his shadow deep in light.

THE WILD LIFE OF
GLEN MORE

By SETON GORDON

Glen More stands high. Loch Morlich on its low ground is over
1,000 feet above the level of the distant sea, and the summit of
Cairn Gorm, which rises in a comparatively gentle slope from the
loch, is 4,084 feet high. The district, besides its elevation above the
sea, is almost at the heart of the Scottish Highlands, midway
between the North Sea and the Atlantic, and thus more nearly
approaches the Continental climate than most parts of Scotland.

Gone are the days when elk, bear, wild boar and wolf roamed the
forest of Glen More. The red deer was with them, and it has remained and indeed increased in numbers. In summer the red deer
are in the high corries of Cairn Gorm; in winter they find shelter
among the old pines of the old Caledonian Forest which at one time
stretched in an almost unbroken canopy across the Highlands from
western Inverness-shire far into Aberdeenshire. Beneath these old

pines, among great ant heaps where the blaeberry and the cow-berry grow, is to be found in spring the brown, crinkled, edible morel mushroom, which is ready to eat before the birches are in bud.

THE DEER

The male of the red deer is a stag, the female a hind, and the usual Gaelic name for red deer of both sexes is *fiadh*. The stag is antlered, as one of its Gaelic names, *cabrach*, shows, and the antlers are shed each spring. The young horns grow fast, and are full grown in rather less than three months. They are then covered with soft skin known as velvet; until the horns are free of velvet a stag is not considered fit to be shot. The hind (*eilid*) drops her fawn or calf in early June. She chooses usually long, sheltered heather to conceal her baby, but on occasion I have seen a fawn born at a height of 3,600 feet on the Cairngorms. If the little calf is found on the first day of its life, before it has risen to its feet, it will endeavour to make itself invisible by stretching its neck along the ground, laying back its long ears, and half closing its large eyes. Should its human discoverer sit, or stand quietly beside it, the little creature will in a few minutes recover its courage, will lift its neck, cock its ears, and open wide its eyes. Once friendly relations have been established between the two, the difficulty usually is for the human friend to make his or her escape, for the small fawn will do its best to follow its newly made friend and, if it follows far, there is a grave risk that it may not be discovered by its mother when she returns. Red deer, taken early, are easy to tame but the stags sometimes become fierce on reaching maturity. A Highland deerstalker who had reared a stag from infancy was on friendly terms with the animal, which was entirely without fear of the human race. The stag was used to seeing the stalker in plus-fours and a cap. On one occasion the man had to attend a funeral, and donned trousers and a bowler hat. He made his departure without the stag seeing him go: on his return, in the dusk, the stag saw him coming. He did not recognise the stalker in his unaccustomed clothes, set upon him, and killed him. On his gravestone, which I have seen, is an inscription putting it on record that he, the victor over so many deer, himself was killed by a stag.

In Glen More Forest the roe deer (*earb*), much smaller and lighter-footed than his cousin the red deer, is found on the lower ground, among the woods of Scots pine and birch.

SMALLER MAMMALS

The wild cat (*cat*) was almost, if not quite, extinct in this part of the Highlands before the war, but the war years allowed it to return to its ancestral haunts. There is no difficulty in identifying the

GOLDEN EAGLES AT THEIR NEST

genuine wild cat. Its size, the greyness of its coat, its bushy, striped tail, are unmistakable. It has been said, and I think truly, that the wild cat is the one British mammal which has never been tamed. I recall the strange experience I had when walking with a friend late one summer night through the old Caledonian Forest. I was leading at the time, and on coming in sight of the bleached stump of a pine I literally rubbed my eyes. The stump was whitened, and the bark had long since peeled off. In height it was perhaps ten feet, and hollow at the top. From this hollow the bushy tail of a wild cat waved for two or three seconds in the air before it disappeared. The cat evidently had its lair in the hollow tree, and may have been about to issue forth on its night hunting but, hearing or seeing the approach of humans, had darted into its hole. A deerstalker told me of the thrilling encounter he had watched between a golden eagle and a wild cat. The eagle, time and again, stooped at the cat, which on each occasion sprang high into the air to meet the eagle. This fight (or was it play?) continued for the best part of half an hour before the eagle sailed away.

The blue or mountain hare is found on the higher ground of Glen More Forest. Like the stoat (*neas*), the mountain hare in winter

DOTTEREL APPROACHING ITS NEST

becomes as white as the snowy country in which it lives. The fox, too, is found right up to the highest tops, and increased greatly during the war years. The marten cat or pine marten (*taghan*) is extinct in this part of the Highlands although it is still found in the remote north west districts. The otter (*dobhran*) is found on the streams and lochs and the badger (*broc*) is scarce, butnot unknown.

BIRDS

Bird life in the Forest Park is varied and interesting. The grandest of our British birds, the golden eagle (*iolaire*) is sometimes seen sailing high above the forest, or performing breath-taking dives for sheer joy in its power of flight. The rush of the eagle's wings as it falls headlong earthward before mounting once more to its former level sounds like the thunder of an express train in the Spey valley far beneath. It is hoped that all who find enjoyment in this forest park will help to protect the golden eagle, its eyrie, eggs and young. We can ill afford to permit this, the king of birds, to share the fate of the sea eagle which has become extinct within living memory. The food of the golden eagle is rabbits and mountain hares, ptarmigan and red grouse. But sometimes the great bird kills

A PAIR OF GREENSHANKS CHANGING OVER THEIR NESTING DUTIES

unexpected birds and beasts. On one occasion a number of grey crows were lying, plucked, in an eyrie, and I have more than once seen the remains of a stoat. A pair of eagles which my wife and I studied at close range from a hide day after day in the Cairngorms used to bring red squirrels as food for the eaglets, and we often wondered how they were able to catch those agile creatures. The eaglets were none too fond of squirrel as an article of diet: the squirrel's tail was left until the end. The tail was then swallowed whole, long fur and all, with a comical expression of distaste on the eaglet's face. It should be mentioned that squirrels were not fed to the eaglets until the young birds were feathered, and were able to tear up the food for themselves.

The golden eagle lays two eggs and it has been my invariable experience that one egg hatches into a young male, the other into a young female. In birds of prey it is the female which is the larger of the pair, and this difference in size is apparent in the golden eagle at a very early stage. Eaglets, in the early, downy stage are most pugnacious. The eyrie, built on a very old Scots pine, to which squirrels were brought, contained a young female which spent a large part of the day in tormenting her small brother. When he was asleep she would sometimes toddle unsteadily across to him and deal him a strong and deliberate blow on the head or back of the neck with her already formidable bill. At the aggressor's attack the

CRESTED TIT AT ITS NEST HOLE

eaglet would leap to his feet and run from her, she following more clumsily. Since she was overfed, and he was half starved, he was able to run faster than she, and it was this that saved his life. I have found a dead eaglet in an eyrie, and it is not an infrequent occurrence that one of the two eaglets hatched mysteriously disappears during the early weeks. In the light of our experience at this eyrie I have no doubt that it has been killed. It was noteworthy that these attacks were made only during the early stages of the aggressor's life: after the eaglets had begun to grow their feathers they lived together in harmony. When the golden eagle breeds in the pine forest zone the eyrie is invariably built with a platform of green pine shoots, which the eagles tear from the trees, and, as invariably, the eggs repose on a lining of blades of *Luzula sylvatica*, the great wood rush.

Like the eagle, the fierce peregrine falcon is sometimes seen in Glen More Forest. In olden times the goshawk had her eyrie here, and the osprey bred on Loch Morlich. Though the goshawk has vanished, the osprey still returns occasionally, and in 1958 it actually nested near the Sluggan Pass. Unfortunately the nest was robbed, but in 1959 another nest was made near Loch Garten, and for the first time in 106 years a brood of ospreys was successfully reared in Scotland. Several other broods have been reared since then, though the nests have needed close protection.

Red grouse (*eoin ruadha*) are found on the Glen More Park up to

33

an elevation of 3,000 feet above the sea; above that height, up to the highest tops, the ptarmigan takes the place of the grouse. Ptarmigan (*tarmachan*) in winter assume a pure white plumage and to see these birds amid snowy wastes is to realise how effectively they harmonise with their surroundings. Until the early days of May, flocks of snow buntings, lark-like birds with black and white plumage, may be seen on the Cairn Gorm plateau—they then fly north to their nesting grounds in Greenland and Spitsbergen. Soon after the snow bunting leaves the high hills the dotterel, of old called the foolish dotterel (*an t-amadan mointich*, The Fool of the Moss) because of its remarkable tameness, arrives. The dotterel has wintered in Israel, in warmth and sunshine, yet this wader, which calls to mind a miniature golden plover, nests amid the great snowfields of the high Cairngorms where in June the drifts piled up by winter storm still lie many feet deep. The golden plover (*feadag*) occasionally nests as high as the dotterel's haunts, but is usually found at lower levels, where the whaup or curlew (*guilbneach*) sings his mournful song during the months of spring and early summer. That long-legged wader the greenshank is sometimes seen feeding in a forest loch, or travelling high in swift flight from one part of the forest to another; occasionally it nests here.

The sandpiper and the goosander haunt the waters of Loch Morlich, and in the old pine woods the brightly plumaged crossbill, the elusive crested titmouse and its relations the blue, coal, willow, long-tailed and great tits nest. In May the willow warbler sings plaintively from the pendulous birches and the voice of the cuckoo or gowk (*cubhag*) carries far across the pollen-scented forest. There the siskin nests, and the redstart flirts. The greater spotted wood-pecker, with its long brick-red tail, drums with its beak against the stem of some ancient pine, white and lifeless, and in certain clearings of the forest blackcocks (*coileach dubh*) each morning at dawn display with excited bubbling cries. The capercailzie haunts the area of old pine forest, although the felling of old pines has sent many of these birds, of which one of the Gaelic names is *capull coille*, elsewhere. The hedge sparrow nests in the junipers, which here may reach a height of fifteen feet, with tree rather than bush form, and on May days the songs of tree pipit and chaffinch mingle with the subdued notes of the dipper, perched on some moss-grown boulder of a rushing hill burn.

The raven (*fitheach*), which had disappeared from the Glen More area before the 1939-45 war, has reappeared on Upper Strath Spey. The grey or hooded crow (*feannag*), known usually in the Highlands as the "hoodie", maintains its numbers despite the fact that on every gamekeeper's list it is "public enemy number one". The grey crow is an intelligent bird, and much persecution over many years has made it crafty and difficult to entice into the ambush that is so often laid for it. The oyster catcher (*gille bride* or *trilleachan*) enlivens Loch Morlich with its shrill music, and the ringed plover, an attractive bird, is sometimes heard here.

FISH

Salmon (*bradan*) spawn in some of the streams of the forest, and most of the lochs contain trout (*breac*)—and some of them pike (*geadas*). Char (*tarragan*) occasionally take the angler's fly, but these brightly coloured fish keep usually in deep water.

I do not know whether it has been established which is the highest-lying loch to hold trout in the Scottish Highlands. I believe it is Loch Etchachan, which is on the high shoulder of Ben Macdhui, in sight of Glen More Forest Park. Loch Etchachan lies 3,100 feet above sea-level, and is usually frozen until May. It holds trout which are thin, but are sometimes of considerable size. At one time the fishing on Loch Etchachan was considered good enough for a boat to be carried up to the loch. The boat has disintegrated but the trout remain.

RECENT CHANGES IN THE FAUNA

The effects of the 1939-45 war, when Norwegian troops trained in the Forest of Glen More, persisted for many years. On the foot-hills and in the glens of the Cairngorms, great areas of Scots fir, of the old native stock, were felled. The birds of the forest—the capercailzie, the crested tit and others, suffered a rude shock, and for a time it looked as if bird life would be adversely affected—as indeed it was. But Nature is resilient, and no lasting harm has come to the wild life of the hill country, which has long been unusually rich, although the oyster catchers which nest on the gravelly shore of Loch Morlich find the number of visitors embar-rassing. The oyster catcher arrives from the coast early in March, and makes its way slowly from the Moray Firth, following the course of the Spey. It is heard at Aviemore at night some time before it is actually seen. It is likely that scouts from the coast or from their temporary halting places along the lower reaches of the Spey travel west high above the river to see whether snow and frost have left the uplands and then return with their report. I have myself seen common gulls make a flight to a high loch in the hills in mid-April and on finding their nesting site frozen return to the low ground with much peevish clamour. Oyster catchers are delightful birds, and they can on occasion be very friendly. During the summer of 1955 an oyster catcher each evening visited the lawn of the Laird of Rothiemurchus, where it fed along with the local blackbirds and thrushes and when disturbed by a passer-by or by a dog almost at once returned to its search for worms. I think this is one of the birds which has increased in the district.

The golden eagle is now considerably scarcer in the area than it was twenty years ago. Ptarmigan, as a result of unfavourable seasons during the war years and also because of their disturbance, and probably shooting, by armed forces during those years were, at the end of the 1939-45 war, scarcer than I had ever known, but they increased in a remarkable manner during the following five years. The June blizzards of 1953 and the May blizzards of 1955, both coming at the nesting season, again reduced their numbers.

I have mentioned the extensive felling of trees during and immediately after the war years and its effect on wild life. But the scene is now changing as the young woods planted by the Forestry Commission are slowly approaching maturity. Planted woodlands are seldom so favourable to wild life as natural woodlands, and so it is a pleasure to see that the Commission is fencing off certain areas from deer, in order that the old native Scots firs may be able to regenerate themselves. Now that most of the Cairngorm area forms a large Nature Reserve, I would suggest that, before it is too late, many areas in the glens and elsewhere should be fenced in where a few of the native stock of Scots firs are still found. Otherwise it is almost certain that, in the Forest of Mar area especially, large areas in some of the most beautiful tree-bearing glens will in time become treeless. The Nature Conservancy already have this problem in mind.

RIENDEER BORN AT GLEN MORE BELOW CAIRN GORM
The males have much larger antlers than the cow and her calf

THE HERD OF REINDEER

By Dr. ETHEL JOHN LINDGREN

Field-glasses are trained on the high corries and the fringes of Glen More Forest in the hope of catching a glimpse of Britain's only herd of reindeer (*Rangifer tarandus*). Enigmatic, neither wild nor tame, the 'bulls', 'cows', 'calves' and gelded 'oxen' are much discussed by scientists, veterinary surgeons, naturalists, broadcasters and the press.

Antlers and bones of reindeer have been found in prehistoric caves and on sites excavated even in southern England, but the last reindeer known to have survived the mediaeval chase were hunted by Vikings in Caithness, according to the Orkneyinga Saga, about 800 years ago. A few which were imported as curiosities in the 18th and 19th centuries, apparently without herders, soon disappeared.

In 1947 Mr. M. N. P. Utsi saw the Cairngorms through a late April snowstorm and diagnosed "reindeer country". Lichens, overlooked by many experts because they are often hidden beneath short heather, proved so abundant that he resolved to bring selected

37

animals from his own Swedish Lapland herd to Scotland. Official obstacles were surmounted through the representations of the Reindeer Council of the United Kingdom, founded in 1949, and the Scottish Council (Development and Industry). Small consignments arrived, 1952-1955, from Norrbotten via Narvik, travelling over a thousand miles by lorry, train, boat and horse-box. In 1961 a bull and some cows were brought from southern Norway to forestall inbreeding. On these five journeys no animal was lost or injured. Nevertheless close confinement, which was continued during four weeks' quarantine in the urban air of Edinburgh, Glasgow or Newcastle-on-Tyne, told heavily on the wide-ranging reindeer. Regulations imposed for the experiment restricted the first arrivals to fenced ground for nearly two years, and in the hot, wet summer of 1953 there were casualties from fly-strike. However observation of the reindeer gradually dispersed official and private fears.

From the beginning of 1954 the Forestry Commission allowed the herd to use the splendid expanse of lichen-covered slopes south and east of Loch Morlich, up to the sky-line. The big forest fire of 1960 unfortunately depleted both the fenced grazing below Moormore, generously leased in 1951 by Lt.-Col. J. P. Grant, M.B.E., of Rothiemurchus, and the lichen cover on a small fenced plantation in Queen's Forest which had been chosen in 1953 to demonstrate that conifers are not harmed by reindeer.

The Department of Agriculture at Edinburgh recognised in 1956 that reindeer could live and breed in Scotland. No special restrictions remained; the Reindeer Company Ltd. was therefore free to try to build up a herd well adapted to local conditions. By Christmas 1964 it consisted of 29 head born at Glen More (12 of them representing the second or third generations) and 5 of the Scandinavian imports. The natural increase has been partly offset almost every year by one or two accidents, by the elimination of animals not required for breeding, and recently by the slaughter of oxen for meat. Reindeer occasionally vanish without trace. Yet the slow, steady rise in numbers of the native herd was not interrupted until 1964, when dogs worried the cows before the calving season. Dogs off the lead are a serious menace to the herd.

Research is a major objective and extensive records have been kept. A new spraying technique has minimised the insect problem; the de-horning of a few male calves and stilboestrol implants on some adult animals were undertaken experimentally to add weight, which in a Scottish bull has reached 21 stone 1 lb. A cow has calved several times since a caesarean operation, probably the first ever attempted on a reindeer.

Since Mr. Nicholas Labba's return to Norrbotten in 1954,

herding has been carried out by Highlanders or Englishmen, closely supervised by Mr. Utsi when he is on the Reserve. The Reindeer Council's desire to spread knowledge of reindeer farming within the Commonwealth is best fulfilled when visitors accompany Mr. Utsi or the herder to inspect the animals, perhaps helping to corral them or shift the herd to new pasture. Sometimes an ox carries equipment or provisions on a pack; in winter there may be time for sleighing. Arrangements can usually be made at Reindeer House, a stone-faced lodge east of the Glen More camp site, or by letter to the Company's administrative office, Newton Hill, Harston, Cambridge. Reindeer bulls should not, of course, be approached closely in October, when they are in rut.

The lichen *Cladonia rangiferina* is well-known as "reindeer moss", but *Cl. alpestris*, *Cl. sylvatica*, other ground lichens and several rock and tree lichens are important elements in reindeer fodder, in Lapland and the Cairngorms. Red deer have never been reliably reported to eat lichens unless they are starving, and there is little overlap in diet, although reindeer also enjoy the first green grass of spring.

Reindeer meat, fresh or smoked, is a popular food not only among the peoples of the circumpolar regions but throughout Scandinavia, in Germany and the United States, always fetching a good price. In 1951-1952, 400 tons imported by London firms were quickly bought by the general public. Reindeer hide tans to a suède-like finish for luxury gloves and hand-bags. Skins with the hair on, simply stretched and dried, make the warmest of ground sheets for explorers. Reindeer milk is delicious and as rich as cream. To acquire a pair of reindeer antlers is often a tourist's dream, but most of those in Scotland are still kept for exhibition and study.

BIBLIOGRAPHY

The Composition of the Milk of the Reindeer. ASCHAFFENBURG, R., GREGORY, MARGARET E., KON, S. K., ROWLAND, S. J., and THOMPSON, S. Y. 1962. *Journal of Dairy Research*, vol. 29, pp. 324-328.

Controlling Scotland's Wild Deer. STEPHEN, DAVID. 16 May 1963. *Country Life*, pp. 1102-1103.

The Future of Reindeer in Scotland. UTSI, M. N. P. 1957. *Oryx*, vol. 4, pp. 39-42.

Hypoderma diana (Diptera, Oestridae) and *Lipoptena cervi* (Diptera, Hippoboscidae) as Parasites of Reindeer (*Rangifer tarandus*) in Scotland with Notes on the Second-Stage Larva of *Hypoderma diana*. KETTLE, D. S., and UTSI, M. N. P. 1955. *Parasitology*, vol. 45, pp. 116-120.

The Influence of Man on Animal Life in Scotland. RITCHIE, JAMES. C.U.P. 1920.

A Little Lapland in the Heart of the Cairngorms. MOORHOUSE, SYDNEY. 26 January 1963. *Scotsman Week-end Magazine.*

Reindeer in the Cairngorms. UTSI, M. N. P. 19 March 1964. *Country Life.*

Reindeer in Scotland. WATSON, GEOFFREY. 1964. *Wild Life Observer,* No. 8, p. 13.

Reindeer in the Scottish Highlands. 1956. *Veterinary Record.* vol. 68, p. 278.

Rudolph the Camera-shy Reindeer. November 1964. *Climber,* vol. 3, No. 1.

The Sleigh Team of St. Nicholas. TEGNER, HENRY. 19 December 1963. *Lady.*

REINDEER BULL IN RUT ON AIRGIOD MEALL
This bull has been marked with red to distinguish it from a stag in the stalking season

When in the years of war the lumbermen have come to our forest
And tossed aloft the pigeon's wing and unhoused the squirrel,
And driven raw wounds into the golden-brown pines,
And dragged the fallen and humiliated timber at the rear of the arbitrary tractor
They have wrought no abiding hurt;
Heather and grass conceal
The axe-made weal,
And in the summer the dragonfly drives his flame across the sawdust embers,
And not a hollow remembers
The commanding rasp of saw, the thunder of ponderous wheel.

FORESTS AND PLANTATIONS

By JAMES FRASER

Glen More Forest is part of an old natural pine forest, which originally extended along the whole Spey valley and into its side valleys and corries up to an elevation of about 1,500 feet above sea-level. By the end of the seventeenth century, the original area of the forest had been much reduced by grazing, by agricultural cultivation, by accidental and wilfully kindled fires, and by a relatively small amount of ordinary forest exploitation work. Other well-known parts of this big forest are Rothiemurchus, Abernethy, Dulnain and Glen Feshie. The small amount of agricultural development in the valley restricted the local demands for timber, and roads were almost non-existent in these forest areas. The survival of a very substantial part of the natural forests to the beginning of the eighteenth century was due to their inaccessibility. But water transport of logs and sawn timber, on the side streams and in the main valley, began at an early date, and probably became important about the end of the fifteenth century, when building of fishing boats and small ships was encouraged by the State. Although pine was the principal tree in the Glen More forest, other trees were birch and alder. The writer of the *First Statistical Account* of the parish (in 1794) draws attention to the handicap imposed on agriculture by the lack of a good local supply of hardwoods.

The earliest recorded use of the Glen More Forest is as a hunting ground, first for the Stewarts of Kincardine, then for the Kings of Scotland, and later for the Dukes of Gordon. The earliest Scottish forest laws were directed by the sporting interests of the forests. At the best, these laws were fairly negative in character, and they probably received as little attention in Glen More as did the later more positive laws directing the planting and regeneration of woods. "Glenmore" in his *Highland Legends*, published in 1789, refers to a special privilege of collecting "torch" wood in Glen More Forest given to the Duke of Gordon's tenants from areas outside Glen More, and this custom was probably much older. The few small agricultural tenants in the clear spaces doubtless enjoyed certain limited rights of pasturing in the forest, and they made full use of them. They also made use of birch bark and alder bark for tanning, and birch bark for roof cover, and they must have supplied their small local needs for timber and firewood from the forest. The peeling of bark from living trees was apparently a common forest offence in Scotland, and it remains common in some northern countries.

The value of timber in the Spey valley, even when reckoned with reference to the low prices of the times, remained small until road and water communications had been improved. The *First Statistical Account* states that in the period about 1677 to 1700, a man might still enjoy the right of harvesting the timber which he could cut with an axe and saw, for the payment of an annual rent of 5s. and a pound of tobacco. The forest accounts of Rothiemurchus Estate, which is close to Glen More, for the year 1766, show that the prices of trees had risen to three merks each (3s. 4½d.) and that the Estate had a fair local trade in trees—logs, deals, backs, flaichs (rough gates or hurdles) and oars. By 1766, several large contracts with timber merchants had been arranged by local landowners. Sir Thomas Dick Lauder, in his notes added to the third edition of Gilpin's *Forest Scenery* (1834), records that, on the Rothiemurchus Estate, the

PINE FORESTS FRINGING THE SANDY SHORES OF LOCH MORLICH

Beyond rises the summit of Cairn Gorm, flanked by Coire Cas; Coire an t-Sneachda is in the centre, and Coire an Lochain to the right

profits during the period of intensive timber working often amounted to £20,000 per year. The figure need not be taken as very exact, but it certainly shows a marked rise in timber values.

The early use of the timber from the Spey valley for local boat building has been mentioned already, and that use continued right down to the middle of the nineteenth century. Although hopes of selling the timber from the district for Admiralty use were raised from time to time, no very big trade appears to have developed. A list of the boats built at the mouth of the Spey is given in the *Statistical Account* of 1794. During the late eighteenth century the manufacture of wooden water pipes was developed. The pine trunks were bored at Rothiemurchus, and shipped to London for use in the New River and similar public water supply schemes.

Big-scale timber operations in the Spey area began about 1622. Nairne refers to one sale by Sir John Grant at that date. The cash involved was £20,000 Scots (£1,666 sterling). A much-recorded transaction is that of the York Timber made in 1728 with Rothiemurchus Estate. The amount of the contract there was £7,000 sterling. The transaction is described by the parish minister of the time as a "stock jobbing business", and the Company as "the most profuse and profligate set that were ever heard of in this corner". The Glen More owner of the time appears to have been interested in the prospects of a profitable deal with the York Timber Company, but without result. Nairne states that several attempts at a sale were made by the Glen More estate before it closed a bargain, in 1784, with Messrs. Osbourne and Dodsworth of Kingston-upon-Hull. The York Timber Company did not complete their payments or their contract with Rothiemurchus, and operations were brought to a close by suitable legal action by the Rothiemurchus proprietor. In spite of the bad reputation of the York Company men, it has been freely admitted that they taught the local men a great deal about big-scale operations, including the construction of big rafts for floating down the Spey. One Aaron Hill has received special mention as the man responsible for the improvement of the Spey rafts.

A few interesting details of the Glen More 1784 contract have been obtained through the kindness of Sheriff Grant of Rothiemurchus. The facts are recorded in a document dated 1808. The felling in Glen More by Osbourne and Dodsworth was restricted to an area of about one fifth of the total timber area. Trees below a certain breast height measurement were excluded from the contract. The working period of the contract was 26 years. The Company worked in perfect harmony with the estate, and the owner of the estate constructed one road for the Company. The Company profited from the experience of the York Company by making greater concentration of the saw-mill work. Towards the end of the contract period, when it became unprofitable for the Company to maintain their big working squads and staff, on account of the scattered nature of the work, an arrangement was made by which the Company gave up its right to any further timber cutting, and they received a repayment of £500. Sir Thomas Dick Lauder, in his work of 1834, records that "The Glen More forest is fast replenishing itself" (by natural regeneration). This record should be read along with the statement (about replanting) of the Ordnance Gazetteer, and along with statements that the area was used as a sheep farm, after the first big felling. It does not appear that any serious reconstruction of the forest was done by planting before the Forestry Commission began its work in 1924.

There are two further exploitation periods to be recorded in Glen More. In the war period 1914-1918, the Canadian Forestry Corps removed a very great part of the natural crop; and again in 1945-

GLEN MORE FOREST IN SPRING

Seen from the north-west corner of Loch Morlich, where the River Luineag
begins. Beyond lie the summit of Cairn Gorm and rugged Coire an
t-Sneachda

1947, war fellings extended over an area of about 200 acres and
removed a volume of about 400,000 cubic feet.

Accounts have been given of the timber floating operations in the
Spey valley by "Glenmore", by the writer of the *First Statistical
Account*, by Nairne and by "A Highland Lady"—Mrs. Smith of
Baltiboys (*née* Grant). The last-named account is a very attractive
piece of descriptive writing. Two distinct stages of the operations
should be distinguished, loose log floating on the side streams and
raft floating on the Spey. The floating on the side valleys was controlled by dams and sluices. The felled logs were drawn by horses
to the side of the burns and there were peeled and allowed to dry
out. When the dams were full and other weather conditions favourable, the logs were pushed into the side burns and conveyed either
to the Spey or to saw-mill sites in favourable positions for working
and further transport operations. In Glen More, there were two lines
of export of this first type—down the Druie and down the Sluggan.

45

In the Spey before the days of the big type of raft introduced by the York Timber Company, the rafts were very simple. When logs were transported, about eight logs were roped together with horse hair ropes. The raft was guided by a man sitting in a *curach*, which was simply a small coracle, and in addition the logs were controlled from the banks by ropes. The *curach* was carried back from the mouth of the Spey or from the saw-mill site by one man. When deals formed the raft, ten to twelve dozen were probably secured by osiers or birch twigs passed through holes in the ends. Those may be the holes referred to by Edmund Burt, an eighteenth-century writer on the customs of northern Scotland, when describing the partition and ceiling boards of Inverness houses. When the big form of raft was developed, the foundation of the raft was made of heavy logs in the form of a brander or grid and those logs were bolted together. Above this framework, other logs or spars or sawn timber were piled and secured. The raft was guided by two men using sweeps or big oars which were left at the point where the raft was broken up. The men of Knockando were the expert tradesmen for the Spey rafting. In the early history of rafting on the Spey, the period was restricted only by the suitable spate periods. By 1808 it is recorded in a Rothiemurchus record that rafting between the dates 15th May and 25th August was prohibited. Fishing interests of the Duke of Gordon were responsible for that restriction.

Written records and other evidence show the progress of the method of working the forest products of the area. The 1794 *Statistical Account* refers to planks prepared by splitting logs with axes and wedges, and by subsequent dressing with adzes and axes. The development of the bigger and more elaborate water-mills was due probably to the big "invading" companies, although small water-mills had been used earlier by local merchants. By 1800 a form of water-worked frame saw had been developed. Later, steam- and diesel-powered mills replaced the water-driven types.

Forsyth, in the account which he has written about Glen More, records that it was converted into a sheep run in the period 1831 to 1841, and that in 1859 the forest was cleared of sheep and was turned into a deer forest. If one remembers and accepts the statement by Sir Thomas Dick Lauder, quoted above, it can be fairly safely assumed that by 1831 natural regeneration had restocked the greater part of the forest following the destruction of the first big fellings. The intensive use of land by sheep can be as destructive to the soil fertility as heather burning, but in Glen More it is not probable that it was ever possible to maintain a heavy stock of sheep. (At all events, the period of intensive sheep use must have been short.) This is due to the severe winter climatic conditions. For similar

NATURAL REGENERATION OF PINE AMID SHINGLE
BESIDE THE RIVER LUINEAG

reasons, the Glen More area could not at any time have maintained a very heavy deer stock. Rabbits are not plentiful in the forest, and they are also unable to reach real destructive numbers on account of the severe winters. Although the destructive powers of sheep are fully appreciated, it is difficult in the case of Glen More to accept the sheep as the full real cause of the failure of natural regeneration from 1834 to the present day.

In 1923 the Glen More property was acquired by the Forestry Commission, which commenced its operations there in 1924. It was realised at the outset that the profitable growth of timber would only be possible on the lower slopes of the hills. An elevation of 1,500 feet, which is roughly the upper limit, in this district, of good Caledonian pine forest, was accepted as the highest contour at which planting for timber production could be undertaken. This meant that some 3,350 acres, or about a quarter of the estate, was regarded as "plantable". The balance of 9,200 acres, consisting of Loch Morlich and the higher braes, was thus left untouched, and in 1948 the creation of the Glen More Forest Park made it more freely available to the public for recreation.

Within the plantable portion the main objective of the Commission's work is here, as elsewhere, the production of marketable timber, and this must govern both the kinds of trees planted and the methods followed in the management of the woods. In some situations a satisfactory procedure is to accept both the native Scots pine and nature's way of regenerating the crop from self-sown seedlings. But although this has been tried at Glen More the results have been variable and on the whole disappointing. Portions of the original pine forests have been preserved, notably around the shores of Loch Morlich, up the Pass of Ryvoan and on the slopes of Airgiod Meall. At the eastern edge of the Park, just north of Loch Morlich and near the point where the Sluggan road joins the direct road from Aviemore, an area has been set aside for natural regeneration of the pines, and since 1930 experiments to encourage it have been carried out in an enclosure; methods tried have included burning heather, digging, and mulching with brushwood. Little success has attended these efforts yet quite a fair growth of young pine is springing up on the heathery slopes between the Allt Mhor and the Ryvoan road. However, on the adjoining property of Rothiemurchus, especially beside the rivers Druie and Luineag, where geological conditions are more favourable than in Glen More, the natural regrowth of the pines is vigorous and promising.

There have been two major phases of planting by the Forestry Commission. 2,100 acres were planted between 1924 and 1933, and over 1,250 acres between 1949 and the present time. Scots pine covers half of this area of plantations, Sitka spruce—one third, and the remainder is made up of lodgepole pine, Norway spruce, European larch, Douglas fir and Japanese larch. The Scots pine is not from the native stock but was grown from seed mainly from estates in North-east Scotland. Nevertheless the Scots pine has proved better than all the other species, though Sitka spruce and lodgepole pine have proved useful additions to the Forest when used with discretion.

The greater part of the early planting has been done simply by "notching" the young trees from a forest nursery directly into the undisturbed surface of the soil. But about 1935 Sir John Stirling Maxwell, Chairman of the Forestry Commission from 1930 to 1932, showed by experiment at Corrour near the Moor of Rannoch that the young trees are given a much better start on these wet peaty moorland soils if they are planted through an overturned sod so that they can root in well drained soil. This work was first done with spades, but later it was found that the ploughing up of long strips of sod provides a well drained soil for the young trees, while the groove formed by the plough serves as an open drainage channel. This procedure has now become standard practice wherever the Forestry Commission afforests peaty or heathery moors, and a considerable stretch of ground to the north of Glen More Lodge has been treated in this way.

It is well worth a visit since it enables one to compare the rapid growth of young trees on ploughed land with the far slower start they have made elsewhere in this forest, when planted by conventional methods or arising from self-set seeds. Indeed, measurements have shown that natural pine seedlings often take twenty years to become two inches thick at ground level! Other features worth noting are the very variable form of the native pines, and the peculiar cylindrical shape assumed by many Sitka spruce trees, probably because their lower side branches are so often nipped back by spring frosts.

An experiment in afforesting the ground above the existing limits of the pine forest was commenced in 1930. A number of species including lodgepole pine, the European mountain pine (*Pinus mugo*), Norway spruce, Sitka spruce, and the American white spruce (*Picea glauca*) were tried, as well as the native Scots pine. The effects of draining and fertilizing on these species were studied, and there are indications that trees can be grown successfully at the higher elevations and on the poorer soils. Lodgepole pine has been notably successful under the most severe conditions. This trial plantation may be reached by diverging from the main Cairn Gorm road, towards the left, where the road itself leaves the course of the Allt Mor burn; it lies between that stream and the Allt na Ciste, just above the old pines, at an elevation of 1,600 feet, and can be found by striking 400 yards east of the first hairpin bend above the deer fence.

Although the growth of timber has generally been slow at Glen More compared with that at forests in kindlier situations, certain of the older plantations have already reached the stage where thinning out is needed. The current yield from thinnings amounts to 10,000 cubic feet of timber each year, and this is sure to increase as more woods reach their thinning stages. When the new paper pulp mill at Fort William starts to operate in 1966, about 22,000 cubic feet of timber will be harvested annually. The work of planting, tending the trees, and harvesting their timber, provides continuous employment for some fifteen men. Eight houses have been built to accommodate some of the workers and the rest come from surrounding districts. The timber houses, of Finnish design, erected near the camping ground, deserve notice as showing how wooden buildings can prove satisfactory under a harsh climate.

In order to get the timber out and to provide ready access to all parts of the forest in case of fire, a system of forest roads, extending to 20 miles and including a sturdy bridge, has been constructed by the Commission's engineers. Although these roads are not open to cars, walkers are free to use them; but the Commission reserves the right to close them at times of extreme fire hazard.

There are two dangers to which these valuable young woodlands are exposed, and the co-operation of visitors is sought in reducing the risks to a minimum. The deer that come down from the heights in winter can do very severe harm by grazing and browsing the young trees, and the whole of the planted area has been surrounded by a deer-proof fence, six feet high. Visitors are asked to co-operate by leaving the gates closed or else by using the stiles provided on certain of the footpaths. Both the trees and the heathery vegetation in and around the forest are very inflammable, and in one disastrous fire in 1942 on the south side of Loch Morlich over 200 acres of young trees were lost. During Whitsunday, 1960, another fire, undoubtedly caused by a discarded cigarette, burned down 314 acres of fine timber. Therefore exceptional care must be taken always with matches, tobacco, or fire in any form. Camp fires may only be lit within the camping grounds or at the picnic point beside Loch Morlich. In dry weather conditions become extremely hazardous and the forester in charge may prohibit fires entirely. Should a forest fire unfortunately arise, the co-operation of visitors is requested both by promptly reporting it to the forester's office behind the Lodge ('phone Aviemore 271) and in giving what help they can in putting it out. Fire beaters will be seen at several strategic points, while other equipment is kept in readiness close to the forest office.

The forestry programme at Glen More is part of a great scheme to establish productive woodlands throughout Great Britain which will eventually give us about one third of all the timber we need. About half of this forested area will be in Scotland and the traveller in his journeys to and from Glen More is sure to see many other young forests, particularly in the valley of the Tay. Current planting programmes provide for 30,000 acres of new forests in Scotland every year.

The biggest Commission project in Strath Spey is at Inshriach near the foot of Glen Feshie, where 3,300 acres have already been afforested, and a further 2,900 acres will eventually be planted up.

The forester in charge at Glen More will gladly assist visitors who wish to see any particular aspect of the work there. Information regarding other forests in the North of Scotland may be obtained from the Conservator whose office is at 60 Church Street, Inverness.

In 1935 the ancient forest of Glen More received the title of the Queen's Forest, in commemoration of the Silver Jubilee of King George V and Queen Mary, as recorded on the memorial stone of local granite which was set up at the head of the Sluggan Pass.

The total area of the Forest Park is 12,500 acres, nearly 20 square miles; 3,350 acres have been planted with tree crops, and 9,200 acres of the more high-lying land is regarded as unplantable and will probably always remain as it is today.

The Park is 7 miles long from north to south, and 3½ miles wide. The 22-mile walk around its circumference passes over 14 named summits, all of which may be seen from Glen More Lodge.

All the area lies at more than 1,000 feet above sea-level. The highest level at which a self-sown pine seedling has been found is 3,000 feet.

The whole forest is covered by a short-wave radio system, so that the staff, when travelling on duty, are always in touch with their main office.

THE SAILING LESSON, LOCH MORLICH

51

SAFETY ON THE MOUNTAINS

By A. L. McClure

Chief Constable of Inverness-shire

It is, perhaps, true to say that in no part of the world is there greater emphasis on sport and all forms of recreation than there is in this comparatively small country of ours. Indeed, our measure of success in this field of competition compares favourably with the best in the world. The determination to win, the desire to prosper, the zest for excitement and the love of pleasure, are all unmistakable characteristics of the British race. The spirit of adventure is self-evident, and, in fact, so manifest on occasions as to be inclined to displace prudence in the face of danger. This has not been more clearly illustrated than in the terms of cost to human life and limb in mountaineering accidents.

Mountaineering is undoubtedly one of the finest forms of recreation this country has to offer its youth: exhilarating, stimulating, challenging and—unfortunately what is not always appreciated—fraught with danger. Contrary to the somewhat hackneyed explanation, mountains are not climbed 'because they are there'; rather, they are climbed because they have so much to offer. It is not always realised that in winter or summer these mountains demand the utmost respect if they are not to exact their grievous toll of life.

The number of accidents on our Scottish mountains within recent years has been quite disturbing, particularly in the knowledge that most of them need not have happened had there not been such a flagrant disregard for the simple laws of safety. This needless waste of young lives is viewed with serious concern, to say nothing of the heavy strain on Police man-power and other volunteer services in the discharge of both official and moral responsibilities to mankind. It is singularly regrettable that such a high percentage of those who fall victim to the perils of mountaineering are students from colleges and universities throughout the country; people of promise, a high standard of intelligence and education, whose potential contribution to society our country can ill afford to lose.

In Scotland, especially, in accordance with the constitutional laws of the country, mountain search and rescue organisation is officially the responsibility of the Police. In the organisation the

Police are ably assisted by other interested bodies, such as local mountain rescue teams, Royal Air Force Mountain Rescue Teams, T.A. volunteers from the 4th/5th Battalion, The Queen's Own Cameron Highlanders, the Ambulance Services, the British Red Cross Society, the Mountain Rescue Committee, and other interested bodies who give their services unstintingly in whatever capacity they are best suited.

Much is being done to educate the unwary in the etiquette of mountain safety, such as periodical 'Police Call' programmes on both sound and television broadcasts, the exhibition of suitable

SKI-ING ON AN EASY SLOPE NEAR THE CAMP SITE

Along the far ridge from left to right are Coire Laoigh Mor, Coire na Ciste, the Cairn Gorm and the Fiacaill a' Choire Chais above Coire Cas

posters and the dissemination of other advisory propaganda. Yet it continues to be an up-hill task to convince some people of the importance of being equal to the challenge before it is accepted. It is distressing to find that the sound advice so freely and seriously given should be all too often ignored, and with such tragic results.

As Chief Constable of Inverness-shire, in which County there has been a most disturbing death-rate on the mountains during the last decade or so, I earnestly appeal to every young climber, and also to every young person who very soon may discover the magnetic power of the mountains, and for whom this article is intended, to treat the advice it contains as being a very personal message, and not at all to be dismissed lightly as being directed at someone else.

The rules of the game are but the basis of good, common sense, and are set out as follows:

GENERAL FITNESS
1. Mountaineering is an arduous and, sometimes, exacting sport, demanding physical fitness and mental alertness of no mean order. Do not think that you are fit for mountaineering if you have just vacated your office chair, or are just having a break from your studies. Mountaineering is a real test of stamina, and you should leave it severely alone unless you are physically fit for it.

EXPERIENCE
2. Learn as much as possible about mountaineering by reading books and asking questions of experienced climbers who will be delighted to tell you much more than the scope of this article permits. You will discover that there is much to learn.

CLOTHING AND FOOTWEAR
3. It is common knowledge that people have died on the mountains (a) because of inadequate clothing and (b) because of unsuitable footwear. You must provide for your protection against both weather and ground conditions.

4. Bear in mind that when the temperature is just on the freezing line at sea level there will be a minimum of 15° of frost on the summit of Ben Nevis, and perhaps as much as 28°. Make adequate provision for warm, windproof clothing, including gloves and headgear.

5. Suitable footwear is of the utmost importance. Either nailed or vibram-soled *boots* are recommended, preferably the former for all-round conditions, especially if you are to encounter ice or wet, slippery rocks. Your climbing boots should be a size larger than you wear in normal footwear, as this will enable you to wear two pairs of woollen stockings.

6. As this article is intended for the guidance of the uninitiated it does not cover all the paraphernalia that is usually carried by the expert climber. To begin with you should limit your equipment to the bare necessities. An ice axe is essential if you encounter snow-slopes; but remember you must know how to use it. Its most important use is to prevent you crashing to destruction!

7. Any ideas of ambitious rope-work should be dispelled until you have had the benefit of expert instruction. You must carry a map, compass, whistle, torch and watch; but if you do not know how to use your map and compass you might as well leave them at home! It may sound incredible, but it is still true that many mountaineers have no idea how to use their map and compass. A slight error in navigation could lead you to destruction!

FOOD

8. Never attempt any form of mountaineering without a good supply of food. It is better to carry concentrated foods which do not encumber you unduly. Glucose, chocolate and fruit are high on the list. The main thing is to ward off the pangs of hunger.

NUMBERS IN PARTY

9. It is nothing but the height of folly to attempt any form of mountaineering alone. Go mountaineering alone and you are in gross breach of etiquette! There should never be less than three members in a mountaineering party so that, in the event of mishap, one member stays with the injured party while the third summons assistance.

10. Make sure that you have at least one experienced climber in the party, and do not make any stupid suggestions to him as to what should be done in the face of impossible conditions. Remember never to separate except in emergency.

PLANNING

11. You must plan carefully whatever it is you intend doing on the mountains. In winter time you must not forget to take into consider-ation the amount of daylight available. Having made your plan you must stick to it, or else abandon it and return home, but never abandon it in favour of something else without telling someone. There have been instances of climbers intimating their intention to climb in a certain area and, without further notice, changing their plan to something else. The inevitable consequences of such thoughtlessness in the event of mishap would be that searchers would be despatched to the area intimated, while you might be dying of exposure and injuries only a matter of half a mile away.

GLISSADING

12. From records of accidents occuring on the mountains it emerges that many have been due to careless glissading, such as glissading in misty conditions when snow slopes reach out over sheer cliff faces, and glissading in snow which is too soft, and in which it is impossible to break one's fall with an ice axe. Glissading calls for every possible care.

CONCLUSION

13. If all young climbers and, indeed, some of those who have already gained a measure of experience, and, perhaps, escaped mishap only by the Grace of God, pay attention to their more experienced elders, refrain from tempting providence, and obey the simple, commonsense rules of the game, then we may look forward with confidence to an encouraging fall in the graph which has signified so much grief, entailed so much expenditure of physical effort, and incurred so much expense in the past.

THE CAMPING GROUND IN SPRING
The far hills are the Cairn Gorm, Cairn Lochan and Creag an Leth-Choin

Where essential silence chills and blesses
And for ever in the hill recesses
Her more lovely music broods and dies . . .
For there among the flowers and grasses
Only the mightier movement sounds and passes,
Only winds and rivers, life and death.
—Stevenson

THE CLIMBING GROUNDS
OF THE PARK

By Lord Malcolm Douglas Hamilton

Expeditions into the Cairngorm Mountains involve for the most part long treks over large areas, following sometimes deer or sheep tracks, sometimes wading through heather of varying depths, sometimes scrambling over boulder-strewn territory. But the Ski Road and the White Lady Shieling nowadays provide excellent advanced bases.

If you stand outside Glen More Lodge and look in a southerly direction, the highest point you see if the day is clear will be Cairn Gorm (4,084 feet) the "Blue Mountain". This mountain is only the fourth in altitude of the range to which it has given its name. To the right of Cairn Gorm are three prominent corries with ridges between, and these make the sky-line that you see from Glen More. All along this sky-line there are, as it were, entrance points to the great areas of the Cairn Gorm—Ben Macdhui Plateau, whose great expanse gives unique pleasure to the hill walker and climber. There is, in fact, no greater area of wild country in the whole of Britain than that stretch beyond the sky-line. (See panoramic views, pages 78 to 79.)

There are many easy ways to the top of this plateau for the hill walker who wishes to eschew difficult climbing, but there is also ample scope for climbers who wish to add a bit more spice to their expedition, or who go merely for the sake of climbing. When you first set foot on the summit plateau you see spread in front of you a large area of undulating ground, cut in places by burns which run in summer among what looks like meadows. Ben Macdhui, 4,296 feet and the second highest mountain in Britain, can be seen three miles beyond, and the way to its summit cairn is easy, provided the weather is good and the ground clear of snow. If, however, you first visit this table-land at the height of summer in fine weather, do not be deceived by the peaceful appearance of the countryside, for in winter, when blizzards and gales are frequent, conditions can rapidly become arctic; warm clothing and a knowledge of map and compass are essential. Moreover, wintry weather can come to the high places of the Cairngorms out of the blue at very short notice and at any time of the year.

In general, but with some exceptions—notably in the rather inaccessible Coire Bhrochain on Braeriach—the rock in the Cairngorms is not too good for climbing. It is somewhat friable and loose, with a good deal of vegetation; but in winter the height of the range will generally ensure reasonable snow climbing conditions from November to May.

During these winter months, whether you are intending to climb or not, you should always carry an ice-axe for expeditions into the Cairngorms, and make sure too that you know how to stop yourself with the ice-axe if you fall on a snow or ice slope; because slopes which are perfectly safe in summer can become dangerous under snow and ice conditions if one goes on them carelessly or unprepared. If you should fall, you can easily stop yourself with your ice-axe by grasping it firmly by the head and then turning the spike into the snow; but with no ice-axe at all it is surprising how quickly you can gather speed when sliding down a slope out of control.

The three prominent corries to the right (west) of Cairn Gorm are the places where most of the climbing is done from Glen More. Even if you have no intention of climbing, the corries are well worth a visit on foot because the magnificence of the rock scenery has to be

CLIMBERS IN THE COIRE AN T-SNEACHDA

seen from that viewpoint to be fully appreciated. The eastern corrie, on the left when looking from Glen More and lying just to the right of Cairn Gorm itself, is Coire Cas; the one in the middle is Coire an t-Sneachda; and the western one to the right is Coire an Lochain.

Coire Cas, now easily reached from the White Lady Shieling, is a very safe corrie for the hill walker who wants to start climbing on something steeper, and it is generally used by climbers to give a glissade (which means sliding down a snow slope on your feet, balanced by your ice-axe, when descending after a climb). This corrie often carries a long curved snow-wreath far into summer.

Coire an t-Sneachda is a very beautiful place to visit, winter or summer. The best way to reach the corrie from Glen More is to start by the Cairn Gorm Ski Road and then to contour round to the Fiacaill a'Choire Chais which divides Coire Cas from Coire an t-Sneachda, and aim at reaching the 2,750 foot contour just on the Coire an t-Sneachda side of the ridge. From there you have a gentle and easy pull up into the corrie. When you arrive in the corrie, at a height above sea level of approximately 3,000 feet, you find yourself faced with an imposing array of cliffs and gullies. None of these should be tackled unless you have an experienced mountaineer in charge of the party. If you face the cliffs, to the left you will see slopes, which in winter carry snow, starting on the left-hand side at a fairly gentle angle and steepening up as they meet the rocks. Here there are quite good slopes for beginners in the winter, and slopes which provide easy scrambling on to the summit in the summer. About the centre of the corrie is a massive buttress called the Alladin Buttress, with the Alladin Gulley curving round its left side. The highest point of the corrie is about 3,800 feet, and the ground can be seen to fall away on each side of this rounded top and to descend gradually about 200 feet on each side, during which descent it contains almost the whole corrie. On the right, however, there is a steep rise again past the dip of the Fiacaill ridge to the cairn of Cairn Lochan (3,983 feet) which is right on the edge of the great precipices of Coire an Lochain. On your extreme right you get a very fine view of the Fiacaill Ridge which separates Coire an Lochain from Coire an t-Sneachda. This gives an easy, but quite interesting rock scramble in summer if the ridge is climbed through-out to the summit plateau, and in winter it can present a very good climb indeed. From the corrie on to the Fiacaill Ridge are several good rock climbs, but none of these are safe for beginners unaccom-panied by an experienced climber. To the left of this ridge, and before you come to the main mass of rocks in the Coire an t-Sneachda, you have the lowest point of the top of the corrie. There is an easy scramble in summer up here to the summit plateau from the floor of the corrie, but under winter snow conditions this should not be attempted by the inexperienced.

It is quite safe for a hill walker who is inexperienced as a climber to visit Coire an t-Sneachda at all times of the year, but in winter he does better to retreat the way he came; or he can easily climb up on to the ridge between Coire Cas and Coire an t-Sneachda—the Fiacaill a' Choire Chais.

Coire an Lochain is just as easily approached as Coire an t-Sneachda. You follow the Ski Road to the point where the trees end and the moor begins. Then you take a right-hand path and descend to the Allt Mor, which you cross by a footbridge. You then

AVALANCHE DEBRIS IN THE COIRE AN LOCHAIN

follow the Deer Track on the right bank of the Allt Creag an Leth-Choin until the track peters out, and then take a bee-line for the Coire. It is a corrie of great cliffs and outstanding rocky scenery. It also has an attractive lochan at about 3,000 feet, from which it derives its name. The water of this is always very cold, but can provide a refreshing bathe in hot weather. From the appearance the loch presents for at least six months of the year, when it is generally frozen over, bathing seems somewhat remote!

One of the striking features of Coire an Lochain is a great apron of reddish rock, visible only in summer, which stretches for a height of about 300 feet from near the foot of the upper cliffs almost down to the lochan. This apron is a contributory reason for avalanches which crash down the corrie into the lochan in the winter and spring. The snow is apt to break at the top of this rock apron, and seems to have no difficulty in sliding down the apron to the bottom. Really big avalanches have come down here, and sometimes the snow breaks off clean at a depth of about fifteen feet, and crashes down the corrie in huge blocks. Therefore unless you have a knowledge of the type of conditions that produce avalanches, it is as well not to venture on steep snow slopes in this corrie. There are many rock climbs and snow climbs to be had here, but they are for the experienced climber.

There is an easy exit on the right-hand side as you face the corrie from below, and the route round the top of the corrie to the summit, Cairn Lochan, has some of the finest views in the Cairngorms so

ROCK CLIMBERS NEGOTIATING A CHIMNEY AT CREAG A' CHALAMAIN
Note typical rectangular jointing of rock

far as cliff scenery is concerned. The rocks are piled up in gigantic towers which are riven by gullies and cracks. The great apron of rock down which the avalanches slide in winter can be seen very well in summer from this route.

The only other rock climbing locality in the park that is worthy of mention is to be found in a cleft between Creag a' Chalamain and

the direction of Cairn Gorm, and is very near the summit of Creag a'
Chalamain. This cleft is on the most direct route from Glen More
into the Lairig Ghru. The place, which is well worth visiting just for
the view of the rock scenery, contains a fine little practice rock
climbing ground, giving climbs up to one hundred feet in height
on rock which is, for the most part, sound.

The Cairngorms under all conditions provide a wonderful field
for learning hillcraft, including way-finding and judgment of
distance and time. It is only when the hill walker has had plenty of
experience in these that he should begin to practise the specialised
branches of climbing which are to be found in the places I have
described. If people wish to go in for these they should join one of
the Scottish climbing clubs and learn the craft under experienced
tuition; for rock and snow climbing both require considerable
experience and training.

No matter how long you climb there is always something new to
be learnt and fresh worlds to conquer. The deeper you delve into
the hill secrets the greater will be your reward; but the main thing
is the love of the hills which climber and hill walker share alike. You
want, first of all, a stout heart and body in good training, a knowledge of way-finding in all weathers, well-nailed boots, adequate
clothing and equipment, and food; the Cairngorms will provide all
the liquid refreshment required. If you have no fear of hard work,
the Cairngorms will receive you with open arms and yield their
secrets.

ON THE SOUTH SLOPE OF MEALL A' BHUACHAILLE

Who has seen the glorious elevation of the sun over the shoulder of Ben A'an,
Its whirling brilliance of candelabra and coronal of swords

HILL WALKS IN AND AROUND
THE PARK

By JOHN NIMLIN *and* H. L. EDLIN

The wide mountain background of the Park does not show the bold profiles of many West Coast ranges. Here the contours suggest massive repose. Long, flowing ridges and gently swelling shoulders build up to the serene curves of the summits, and the extensive snow-fields, which sometimes linger until late summer, only tend to increase this air of repose. It is only when the visitor penetrates into their glens and corries that a different aspect is seen. In many of the deeper corries the walls are weathered into great crags and in the wilder glens long scarps of naked granite give depth and grandeur to the scene. Another characteristic of the Cairngorms is the high lochans, the true gems of these mountains, which always seem to be present where the mountains give their most impressive displays. Cradled in the deep basins of glen and corrie, their dark mirrors reflect the changing lights of crag and sky, and an unforgettable sight is the fire which glows in their tremulous depths when the crags are flushed in the sunset.

Other distinctive features of the Cairngorms are the novel effect of snow persisting long beyond its normal season, the wind-scoured sterility of high ridge and plateau and the resulting contrast with the green engirdling forests. To the climber who has been facing the wind and weather of the hilltops the sudden transition into the sheltered forest is delightful. First come the hardiest outliers of the forest, gaunt old pines in sheltered hollows, their boles and limbs braced to meet the harrying winds. Many have long since lost their mail of bark, and the corded fibres under the smooth grey boles stand out like the muscles on ancient Greek statues. Then appear the red boles and tufted green of the living trees and the hilltrack becomes veined with their iron-hard roots.

THREE WALKS WITHIN THE PARK

Each of the following walks can be accomplished within a few hours, though all can provide interest enough for a whole day if taken at a leisurely pace, with halts to enjoy the magnificent views. They are suitable for those who do not wish to climb to the higher hills, and even those who do so will find them a rewarding exercise on days when the weather is unsuitable for the summits. It is assumed in each instance that the reader starts from the Camp Site.

I. TO THE SLUGGAN PASS

Follow the main entrance road along the north shore of Loch Morlich westwards, almost to its western end. You will see on the right a gravel road signposted Sluggan, which you now follow northwards for two miles, climbing slowly through the pinewoods. At the head of the pass a wonderful, unexpected, view opens out north across Strath Spey towards Boat of Garten and the Monadhliath hills. Just before the forest fence is reached, another road strikes off uphill on the left; a stroll up this reveals another grand view south across Glen More towards the Cairngorms.

The return should be made by the same route as far as a signpost on the left indicating Badaguish, once an old croft whose Gaelic name means "a clump of pine trees", but today a group of cottages. Go left to Badaguish, and then bear right through the woods along a forest road that heads straight for the Camp Site, with fine views all the way.

The Sluggan Pass is a right-of-way for walkers to the Aviemore-Coylumbridge-Nethybridge road.

2. TO THE GREEN LOCH AND THE PASS OF RYVOAN

Follow the road that diverges left from the Ski Road just past the Camp Site, and runs below the wooden Forest Workers houses to the Glen More Lodge holiday centre. Proceeding past this large wooden building, the road climbs steadily below young pinewoods until it gains a small, though magnificent, fragment of the primeval Caledonian pinewoods. Soon you will see, on your right, the mysterious blue-green waters of Lochan Uaine, the Green Lochan, which owes its colour to an alga. It has no obvious inlet or outlet, but the water, which is held in a glacial moraine, rarely varies in level.

Beyond, at the head of the pass, you come to the Ryvoan bothy, built originally for shepherds and stalkers, but nowadays used by climbers. The road beyond continues, as a right of way for walkers only, through Abernethy Forest towards Nethybridge.

Retracing the outward road, an interesting diversion is provided by striking off to the right, uphill through the old pines, just before the fence line is reached. Looking backwards, you will enjoy striking and unusual views over the corries of Cairngorm. Eventually you will find a high stile that enables you to cross the deer fence, and on the other side a forest road runs steadily downhill towards the Camp Site.

3. AROUND LOCH MORLICH

Follow the Ski Road, but only as far as the small car park on the flat ground, just beyond the bridge over the Allt Mor burn. There turn off right, and take the first right fork which leads down to the shores of Loch Morlich. Keeping the loch on your right, proceed round its shores until you reach a deer fence, which is crossed by a stile. A path now crosses an attractive expanse of heathland and old pine belonging to the Rothiemurchus Estate, to reach a modern Bridge over the River Luineag, which drains the waters of Loch Morlich. Beyond the bridge, you strike the tarred county road and turn right to follow the north shore of Loch Morlich back towards the Camp Site.

This walk can of course be done in the reverse direction by starting west from the Camp Site along the county road, and keeping Loch Morlich on your left throughout.

CAIRN GORM (4,084 feet) BY THE MAIN TRACK

From the Camp Site cross the concrete bridge and follow the new Ski Road uphill for about $1\frac{1}{2}$ miles, going around two pairs of hairpin bends in succession. On the left of the road, a very large square stone, the Clach Bharraig, will be seen, and just as one draws level with it, a path rising to the left will be found. The path should now be followed almost directly up the ridge, and diverging tracks to the adjoining corries ignored. The going is remarkably easy over short grass and heather, and even towards the summit, where the slope steepens and becomes stonier, the footing remains unusually good.

Alternatively, follow the Ski Road till it ends at the Car Park; then follow the Chair Lift to its summit. From this point the path runs uphill for half a mile, with a cairn every fifty yards. Lazy climbers can use the chair-lift!

THE BEACH, LOCH MORLICH

From the top of Cairn Gorm there is a splendid view of Glen More, Rothiemurchus and Abernethy Forests which surge across Strath Spey to lap the bases of the Monadh Liath hills. But, directly below, the centrepiece of the picture is Loch Morlich, surely one of the loveliest gems to grace a hilltop view in the Highlands. Southwards the view is restricted by the bulky shoulders of Ben Macdhui. A good walker in fair weather can gain the summit of Cairn Gorm from Glen More Lodge in two hours and reach the Shelter Stone beyond in little more than three hours altogether.

CAIRN GORM BY THE NORTH RIDGE

A longer, though somewhat less steep, route to the summit is to follow the Ryvoan track east from new Glen More Lodge for about half a mile. Shortly after passing through the deer fence into the unenclosed pinewoods, strike off to the right and follow a winding burn uphill until the ridge that forms the Park's eastern boundary is reached near Stac na h'Iolaire—the Eagle's Crag. This ridge, at first steep but later gently rising, is then followed due south to Cairn Gorm, passing in turn the three corries—Coire Laoigh Beg,

Coire Laoigh Mor and Coire na Ciste, which lie below on the right. Care must be taken to avoid the steep and often precipitous slopes to the left; and for this reason this approach, which takes some $3\frac{1}{2}$ hours, should be regarded as a fair weather route.

CAIRN GORM TO CAIRN LOCHAN (3,983 feet)

Having gained the summit of Cairn Gorm by either route, an attractive, easy, and perfectly safe walk, in clear weather, is that along the edge of the summit plateau, following the Park's south-eastern boundary as shown on the map. Below to the right will be seen Coire Cas, Coire an t'-Sneachda and Coire an Lochain.

To the left the ground falls steeply away towards Loch Avon hidden in a deep hollow. There is no easy way down into the northern (right-hand) corries which lead towards Glen More until one has worked right round the sheer precipices of Cairn Lochan itself. The best route will then be that described (in the reverse direction) below.

CAIRN LOCHAN BY THE LURCHER'S CRAG (3,448 feet)

First take the Ski Road to a point just beyond the deer fence; then take the right-hand footpath and cross the footbridge to the ruined bothy. A rough track now leads up the right-hand side of the Allt Mor; this is followed to the last one of the three mountain streams converging from the left. This stream, the Allt Creag nan Leth-Choin, may now be followed by a track on its right hand side to the shallow grassy hollow close under the summit rocks of Creag an Leth-Choin, or it may be forsaken at any convenient point for the open ridge on the right which leads directly to the summit of this, the Lurcher's Crag.

Alternatively, in order to view the spectacular rocks of Creag a' Chalamain—the Pigeon's Crag, one may go south-west until, after clambering through that boulder-strewn gap, one sees below one the awe-inspiring defile of the Lairig Ghru. At this point a narrow but quite distinct path will be observed running due south up the northern shoulder of the Lurcher's Crag. Though the slope is steep the footing is good and a line of small cairns may be followed to the ridge.

From either approach a view is soon obtained of the rocky pinnacle of the Lurcher's Crag—Creag an Leth-Choin—which rises sheer from the Lairig Ghru and is a clear landmark from the distant Spey valley. Passing just to the left of the summit rocks, make for a slight grassy hollow and then bear left up a firm rocky slope to the crest of Cairn Lochan.

CAIRN LOCHAN TO BEN MACDHUI (4,296 feet)

From Cairn Lochan proceed south-west until the steep slopes

LOCH AVON AND THE SHELTER STONE CRAG

The Shelter Stone itself lies at the foot of the scree, just to the right of the pointed rock in the foreground, as marked by the arrows. Below the snow wreaths the Garbh Uisge cataract may be seen.

above the Lairig Ghru are neared. Keeping to the ridge above these, go south and descend into the hollow that holds Lochan Buidhe— the Yellow Lochan (3,650 feet). From this saddle two streams descend, the March Burn running west into the Lairig Ghru and the Feith Buidhe running east to Loch Avon. The route now lies across the streams and south up a shoulder covered with broken, though fairly firm, grey rocks; there is no clear path though small cairns may be followed. A small burn is crossed and thence a narrow gravelly path winds up a second shoulder which is topped by the remains of stone shelters built by troops training for arctic warfare. From this point the summit is visible, being marked by an Ordnance Survey reference point, close to which is an indicator to the far-flung view.

On this journey over the battleground of the elements the climber will see many typical features of the High Cairngorms. The granite masses are crumbled into a desert of sand and gravel with the stunted mountain plants holding precariously to their sheltering rocks and hollows, and the cold hill waters are almost invisible in their purity. In such a setting it is easy to imagine that the chill breath of the last ice-age still blows across these fascinating wastes.

As the second highest peak in Great Britain and being moreover more centrally placed in Scotland than Ben Nevis (4,406 feet), Ben Macdhui is without rival for the expanse of territory that it commands—from Sutherland in the North to the Lammermuirs in the Borders. The most impressive features nearby are the peaks of Cairn Toul (4,241 feet) and Braeriach (4,248 feet), ringed with precipices, which may be seen across the deep defile of the Lairig Ghru. Even the exceptionally hot and dry summer of 1955 failed to melt the snowfield in one of Cairn Toul's steep north-facing corries. Although it is debatable whether there *is* perpetual snow in Scotland, these persistent snow beds, which often survive for many years, come very close to it.

Though the ascent of Ben Macdhui presents no real difficulty a sturdy walker should allow nine hours from Glen More Camp Site or twelve hours from Aviemore for the return journey. By making a steep scramble down the course of the Allt a' Choire Mhoir, or else that of the March Burn, the Lairig Ghru may be reached; this provides an alternative return route, although by doing this in clear weather the vast views from the tops are lost by entering the gloomy defile of Lairig Ghru.

THE ISLAND STRONGHOLD OF LOCH AN EILEIN

From Glen More Camp Site take the Aviemore road to the western end of Loch Morlich and then turn left, cross the Bailey Bridge and follow the right-hand track through Rothiemurchus Forest. After some two miles along a clear path, a plainly signposted "cross-roads" is reached. The left-hand path is that to the Lairig Ghru and Braemar, some 23 miles distant. The Lairig Ghru also provides an alternative approach to the Lurcher's Crag and Ben Macdhui, for if one scrambles up to the left about one mile after leaving the last of the pines, one can strike the gap of Creag a' Chalamain and descry the path (previously described) up the north shoulder of the Lurcher's Crag.

Or from Creag a' Chalamain one can make an easy descent back towards Glen More.

If one continues on to the summit of the pass, the remote Pools of Dee, which always hold water though lacking any obvious inlet or outlet, are reached. Just beyond them the Dee itself drops into the pass from the Garbh Choire of Braeriach on the right.

LOCH AN EILEIN AND GLEN EINICH

Returning now to our "cross-roads" in Rothiemurchus Forest we may go north by the right-hand route to cross the River Luineag and join the road from Aviemore not far from Allt nan Caber. This provides an alternative return route to Glen More.

The path that runs straight ahead descends through pinewoods to grassy meadows and the ruins of an abandoned croft beside the Allt Druidh, which it crosses by a high iron bridge. This bridge was erected by the Cairngorm Club in 1912 and it bears a metal plate with the following information:

	Hours	Miles
To Aviemore	$1\frac{1}{2}$	4
To Coylumbridge	$\frac{3}{4}$	2
To Lairig Ghru summit (2,733 feet)	3	$5\frac{1}{2}$
To Derry Lodge	$6\frac{1}{2}$	14
To Linn of Dee	8	18
To Braemar	10	$24\frac{1}{2}$

This bridge is also some 2 hours or $5\frac{1}{2}$ miles from Glen More Camp Site.

It will be noted that the four miles per hour walking rate does not hold good in this rugged country, and for all practical purposes Naismith's formula: three miles per hour for level walking plus half an hour for every thousand feet of ascent, works out admirably. Prospective travellers should find this calculation useful when plotting out routes on a map.

CAIRN LOCHAN CLIFFS

Another factor that the newcomer to these vast uplands should keep in mind, is that their scale can be quite deceptive; what, elsewhere, might be taken for an easy stroll may prove a long, arduous, tramp.

Beyond the bridge a left hand branch in the track leads to Loch an Eilein, one of the most beautiful lochs in the forest. An alternative track bears right down the line of the river to Coylumbridge and thence to Aviemore.

The Loch an Eilein route also provides access to Glen Einich. About three-quarters of a mile beyond the iron bridge, a track which diverges to the left leads through Nature Reserve ground to Loch Einich, which is some six miles away at the head of its steep-sided Glen.

BRAERIACH (4,248 feet)

This splendid peak, the second highest of the Cairngorm range and the third highest in Britain, is best approached from the north by way of the Lairig Ghru path. This is left about two miles north of the summit of the pass before the crags are reached near the

COIRE AN T-SNEACHDA AND THE FIACAILL RIDGE

Sinclair Hut. The long shoulder on the right of the Allt Druidh is ascended to the outlying hill of Sron na Lairig (3,860 feet). Beyond this the way descends to a little col at 3,700 feet (whence it is possible to make a steep descent by a stalker's path to the Pools of Dee). Thence the route to the summit proceeds westwards above the great corries of Braeriach's northern flank.

The view from this hill top shows the more dramatic aspects of the Cairngorms. Not many yards away the hillside plunges over into Coire Bhrochain in a sheer wall of crag, and beyond it the eye will follow the two mile stretch of almost continuous crag which rims the huge neighbouring recess of Garbh Choire, over which the infant Dee takes its first tentative leap towards the distant North Sea. Cairn Toul (4,241 feet), the other dominating point on this massif, fills in much of the foreground view, and across the void of upper Glen Dee is the equally lofty massif of Ben Macdhui, Cairn Lochan and Cairn Gorm. Beyond them is a view of such great width that it is possible to identify peaks in Ross and Sutherland which, on paper at least, seem quite beyond human ken.

GLEN AVON AND THE SHELTER STONE

Beyond the Cairn Gorm ridge lies the deep glen which holds Loch Avon, and it is possible for a stout walker to descend thereto and to return to Glen More over the Saddle in the course of a day —easy of course if he makes use of the chair-lift. However some parties still prefer to bivouac beneath or beside that climber's

74

rendezvous the Shelter Stone. This provides a point from which Ben Macdhui may be ascended or explorations made towards Loch Etchachan.

To reach the head of Glen Avon from Cairn Gorm the least complicated route is south to the shallow depression of upper Coire Raibeirt, from which a stream leads the way through boggy ground to a last steep slope overlooking Loch Avon. This steep section begins some 600 feet above the loch and a descent by the left side of the stream gives the safest line to the track, which runs just a few yards from the loch shore. From now on the scene becomes more impressive with each downward step. A great semi-circle of crags, gullies and foaming torrents hems in the wild boulderstrewn corrie above the loch. As late as July deep snow wreaths may lie in the gullies and, if the mists are low, the glen has an air of brooding grandeur and desolation which is hardly to be equalled in the Highlands.

The level expanse of the loch accentuates the sheer sweep of Cairn Etchachan and the impressive Shelter Stone Crag, which marks the approximate position of the Shelter Stone (Clach Dhian) itself. The Stone is one of the giant rocks which lie a few hundred feet below the great crag, and it is reached by a slanting traverse across the heather flats and stream beds at the head of the loch. Its height above the loch is about 200 feet and it may be picked out by some distinctive patches on its oblong face. A short, low tunnel leads into a small chamber below the Stone, and when the eye adjusts itself to the perpetual gloom, an area is disclosed just big enough to hold about ten reclining people. Heather bedding has accumulated on the floor and the larger holes in the walls have been plugged with stones and turf. For the visitor with sleeping-bag, stove, candles and some experience of "sleeping rough" the chamber provides admirable shelter. It is mentioned in the *Statistical Account* of 1794 as the resort of lawless men and has doubtless served as a mountain refuge for a long time. Nowadays it is frequently visited during the summer months and its visitor's book gives accounts of these journeys.

In winter the glen is usually deep in snow, with Loch Avon a grey expanse of wind-ruffled ice winding into the desolate hills. At this season the chamber may be filled with snow and it takes much hard work with ice-axes to excavate a sleeping place. In such conditions a journey to the Shelter Stone is a first-class mountaineering expedition and the entire party must be fit, experienced and fully equipped.

The route from the Shelter Stone to Loch Etchachan follows a spectacular little track which zig-zags steeply uphill for 600 feet between the rock face of Cairn Etchachan and the lower crags of Beinn Mheadhoin. From the basin of the Loch at 3,058 feet one

SOUTH-EAST

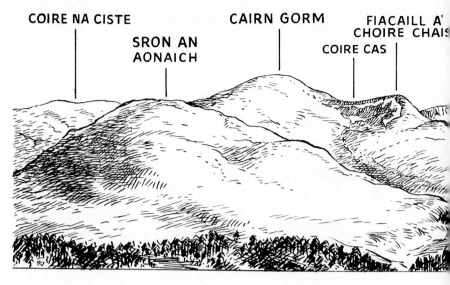

COIRE NA CISTE

SRON AN
AONAICH

CAIRN GORM

FIACAILL A'
CHOIRE CHAIS

COIRE CAS

DUE SOUTH

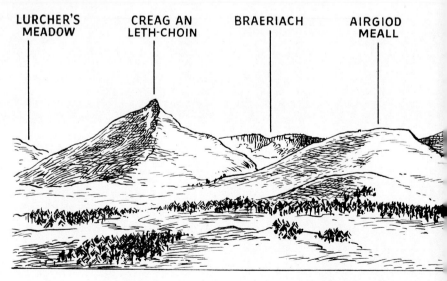

LURCHER'S
MEADOW

CREAG AN
LETH-CHOIN

BRAERIACH

AIRGIOD
MEALL

THE SOUTHWARD PANORAMAS FROM LOCH

The lower portion lies to the right (west)
Castle Hill and Carn Eilrig, then

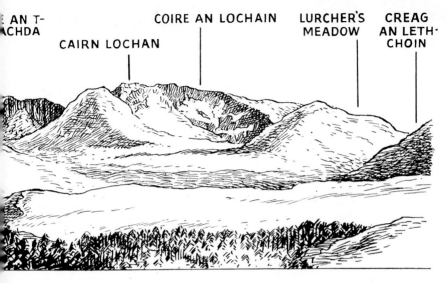

DUE SOUTH

E AN T-ACHDA   CAIRN LOCHAN   COIRE AN LOCHAIN   LURCHER'S MEADOW   CREAG AN LETH-CHOIN

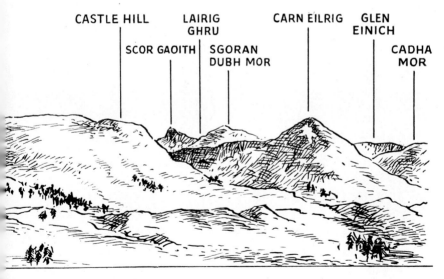

SOUTH-WEST

CASTLE HILL   LAIRIG GHRU   CARN EILRIG   GLEN EINICH

SCOR GAOITH   SGORAN DUBH MOR   CADHA MOR

OUTH HOSTEL—Sketched by *Murray G. Scott*

one. The Lairig Ghru pass runs between
eriach and Creag an Leth-Choin.

has easy access to Beinn Mheadhoin (3,883 feet), Derry Cairngorm (3,788 feet) and to Ben Macdhui itself.

HIGH AND LOW LEVEL ROUTES FROM THE SHELTER STONE

The most direct return to Glen More is by an ascent to the head of Coire Raibeirt and from thence over a little depression in the plateau to the head of Coire Cas. A steep section at the head of this latter corrie is now passed to its right by a scree slope, after which one soon reaches a well-marked path leading to the White Lady Sheiling in the lower corrie, and from thence down the track to the Ski Road.

In bad weather, however, the safest return route is over the Saddle. Retracing the route as far as the burn from Coire Raibeirt the loch-side track is followed for another mile and an ascent of 300 feet is made to the wide pass between Cairn Gorm and A' Choinneach (3,345 feet). Across the pass the route goes north keeping to a little heather track which holds to the side of the Garbh Allt. On the east of the stream rises Bynack More (3,574 feet). At the foot of this long, heathery glen a ruined bothy marks a bridge which carries the main path to Ryvoan. There the scenery changes rapidly when the path dips and swings into the tree-clad defile of Ryvoan Pass and skirts the beautiful Green Lochan (Lochan Uaine) the greenest of the four Green Lochans in the Cairngorms, for it steadfastly reflects the perennial green of its guarding trees. The Camp Site is now only two miles ahead and the lochan comes as a fitting prelude to the pleasant forest lands beyond.

CRAIG GOWRIE—MEALL A' BHUACHAILLE RIDGE

For the visitor with little time to spare the traverse of the hogsback ridge from Craig Gowrie to Meall a' Bhuachaille gives a very comprehensive survey of the Park and its surroundings. Craig Gowrie (2,237 feet) is easily approached from the Sluggan road north-west of Loch Morlich. From its summit to Creagan Gorm (2,403 feet) the going is fairly level, but beyond this intermediate summit there is a dip of about 350 feet and a final rise of 600 feet to Meall a' Bhuachaille (2,654 feet). From this point a descent into the Pass of Ryvoan will suggest itself as an attractive finish to the tour.

———————————

It is well to end a guide to the hill-routes with a note of warning. Due to their height and open contours these hills are subject at times to extreme weather conditions, and weather precepts which hold in other mountain districts are not always applicable here. Severe blizzards may, and frequently do, descend on the summits from September until the end of May, and steep snowslopes with crags and boulders below them may linger into summer to trap the unwary.

To enjoy free wandering, even in summer, climbers should have experience in hill walking, compass-reading and map-reading and it is a good idea to carry some food and clothing reserves for a possible benightment at a high level. In winter and spring every single member of a climbing party should be fully experienced and equipped for hard conditions.

One-inch Ordnance Survey maps are an indispensable part of the equipment. Many of the forest paths are complicated by diverging tracks, and checking-up with the map may save some aimless wandering.

The Cairngorms are great mountains, not only in their bulk but in their wrath; but to the climber who approaches them with due respect they are greater still in their rewards.

GLENMORE LODGE

THE SCOTTISH CENTRE OF OUTDOOR TRAINING
By MURRAY G. SCOTT

Near the eastern border of the Forest Park, almost in the foothills of the Cairngorms, is Glenmore Lodge, the Scottish Centre of Outdoor Training. Built in 1959, it was designed specifically for students undergoing training in outdoor activities.

In 1948, the old shooting lodge of Glenmore, situated one mile to the west, was used by students attending outdoor training courses organised by the Scottish Council of Physical Recreation. General mountaineering was the main activity then, but sailing too was included on some of the courses. Ski-ing was also introduced, and very soon more students than could be accommodated were applying for enrolment on all courses. At this stage, Glenmore was closed for many months of the year, but in 1950 Local Education Authorities in Scotland were invited to send groups of school-children for periods of up to one month, to participate in a new type of education. The subjects taught were way-finding, camping, field studies and, dependent on the season, sailing, canoeing and ski-ing.

The need for a larger building gradually became apparent as these courses increased in popularity. Consequently, in 1958, the Scottish Education Department decided to build the new Glenmore Lodge which was completed and opened within a year. Traditional features however, even in this age of rapid construction, have not been lost, and a subtle use of local stone combined with the use of red cedar cladding for the outer walls, gives a most pleasing effect with the forest and the hills in the background.

Accommodation is for sixty, and throughout the year pupils or students participate in one or more of the activities available. There are courses open to the general public and, depending on the time of the year, students may elect to participate in any activity. On Loch Morlich for example, is found some of the finest small dinghy sailing in Scotland. Winds blowing on to the loch are often so affected by the surrounding hills, that they produce conditions which test even the most skilful sailor. For beginners however, conditions are normally ideal and the combination of sandy shore with forest and mountain background creates a scene so different to coastal areas.

The Glenmore area might be considered unique in that it is possible, at certain times of the year, to participate in either winter or summer activities. No other part of Britain has accessible corries which retain their snow so consistently, year after year, into mid-summer. Indeed, it is not an unusual sight to see the mid-summer skiers heading off to the corries, and even in July the enthusiast can be found on the large patches of snow high in the Cairngorms.

During the Christmas and Easter period, snow and ice climbing and general mountaineering courses are also popular. Some of the finest snow climbing in Britain is found in the gullies of the north-facing corries, and at all times of the year the Cairngorms are ideal for tramping.

College and University groups regularly spend periods at Glenmore, and from this base explore the many interesting regions. At 4,000 feet, the environment is sub-arctic and a study of any aspect of natural history, from this high plateau down to the natural pine forests around the loch shore, at only 1,000 feet above sea level, gives interesting comparisons.

The two Scottish Schools of Physical Education (that for men at Jordanhill, Glasgow, and that for women at Aberdeen), recognising the value of outdoor training in the school curriculum, send their final year students for a week's course. Many other outdoor organisations, too, take advantage of the facilities available and the courses offered.

A fully equipped meteorological station, one of the highest in Britain, is looked after by members of the staff at Glenmore, and day-in, day-out, records of the weather are kept. Although nine years of records does not permit one to give precise averages it would appear, from figures kept so far, that the Glenmore reputation for fine weather is not unjustified. With annual rainfall just over 35 inches, this is one of the driest Highland areas in the country. In winter and spring, much of the precipitation is in the form of snow, and during February, March and April, high pressure systems, spreading south and west from Scandinavia, frequently bring long periods of fine weather.

As much of the work is directly concerned with education, the Scottish Education Department has been closely connected with the Council's affairs. Indeed, the cost of the new Glenmore Lodge was borne entirely by the Department. In return however, they have seen and continue to see the development of a project which started very modestly as an experiment in 1948. Many thousands of students and pupils have participated in courses, and the contribution which Glenmore is making to education and recreation in Scotland will undoubtedly have far-reaching effects.

Further information about courses available may be obtained from:

The Secretary,
Scottish Council of Physical Recreation,
4 Queensferry Street, Edinburgh, 2.

or from:

The Warden,
Glenmore Lodge, Aviemore,
Inverness-shire.

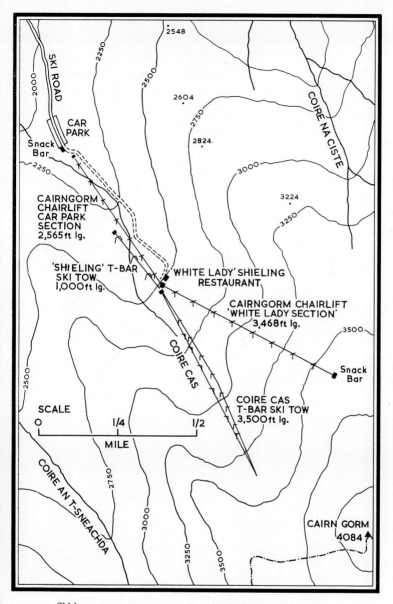

Ski-ing arrangements, car park and refreshments at Glen More

CAIRN GORM SKI LIFT AND THE WHITE LADY SHIELING

SKI-ING IN THE CAIRNGORMS

By ANN FORSYTH TORRANCE

The Cairngorms could fairly be described as Scotland's winter playground; here the snow lies longer and deeper than anywhere else in the British Isles. On average the snow covers more than half of the ground at the 1,000 foot level for thirty to sixty days of the year, and as the elevation increases the total length of snow-lie increases to about 155 days at 2,500 feet, and to 200 days at 4,000 feet. The natural amenities have been known for years to the skier prepared to walk in search of suitable slopes and gullies in which to pursue his sport. In recent years, however, tremendous changes have taken place. Support from hoteliers, and financial backing from Inverness County Council, provided the public access road from Glenmore Lodge almost to the foot of Coire Cas. This was completed in 1960 with a car park for 500 cars, and it is now possible to drive from anywhere in Britain and park on the mountainside.

With the approval of the Forestry Commission, the Cairngorm Winter Sports Board, formed as a non-profit-making organisation by local business men and hoteliers, has taken the hardship from Scottish ski-ing. A successful appeal, spurred on by an anonymous donation of £20,000, enabled the White Lady Chairlift to be built.

84

The T-bar tow in Coire Cas, a trainer tow on the lower slopes of the same corrie, and a rope tow in Coire na Ciste were the next stages of development. It is possible to travel from the car park to the shoulder of Cairngorm, 3,500 feet above sea level, without setting foot to ground and only an easy climb is required to gain the summit at 4,084 feet. The two-section chairlift, in fact, gives immediate or easy access to all the major ski runs in the area.

The White Lady Shieling Trust was responsible for the building of the White Lady Shieling providing shelter, meals and toilet accommodation; they also installed a snack bar at the car park. These amenities are now in the hands of the National Trust for Scotland who have improved the accommodation to include a shop, information desk, buffet and toilets downstairs, and a self-service restaurant, seating approximately 170 people, upstairs. The Shieling also houses a Mountain Rescue Operations room and first aid room equipped with stretchers.

While it is possible to ski from November until July and enthusiasts have been known, in especially favourable years, to ski every weekend from one year to the next, the normal ski-ing season begins in mid-December and usually ends with April. The season can be split in two parts each with its devotees. December, January and February provides, in the average year, a superabundance of snow covering the whole area down and beyond the treeline, so that it is possible to ski almost anywhere, and suitable slopes not usually considered ski runs abound. The weather, however, can be fierce at this time, although glorious days suddenly appear too. The daylight hours are short, and it is not always possible or advisable to ski on the higher slopes. There is compensation though, in the fact that this is a slightly less popular ski-ing time. The lifts and tows are not nearly so busy, there is no coping with large crowds and the snowfall usually ensures great sport on the lower slopes. Tours are possible just above the treeline, and the Sugar Bowl area, situated on the flank of Cairngorm at approximately 1,600 feet, can give excellent ski-ing which is not available later in the season.

March and April are probably the two most popular months; the weather improves and the longer hours of daylight allow more time to be spent on the slopes. The spring snow is excellent. Tours to the outer regions are possible as the chances of sudden storms lessen and the higher slopes are at the peak of condition.

The Cairngorm Plateau affords excellent conditions for ski touring; at the 4,000 foot level, snow lies for fairly long periods and it is usually possible to ski over unbroken snowfields as late as April. A popular tour is to Ben Macdhui (4,296 feet) from Cairngorm, returning by Cairn Lochain and Allt Creag an Leth Choin (The

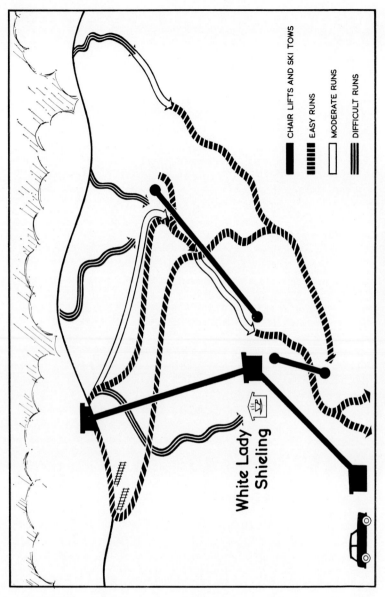

The main ski runs from the Cairn Gorm ridge

Burn of the Lurcher's Crag), a distance of approximately 16 miles with 4,000 feet of downhill touring. Langlauf or ski touring is at the moment pursued by a minority group of skiers, usually skilled ski-mountaineers who know the geography of the area well; it would be an extremely dangerous pastime for the inexperienced. All parties must be led by experienced guides and not in any circumstances should a tour be undertaken lightly. It should be remembered that at 4,000 feet in Scotland the climate is sub-arctic and fierce weather and mist can suddenly envelop the mountains. The skier must, therefore, always be adequately and warmly clad, stay close to the known and popular ski runs, unless equipped with map and compass and the ability to use them, or be in the company of an experienced person capable of leading back down the mountainside in the event of a storm. Never stay for one last lonely run, when everyone else has gone; stay with the crowd, there is always a reason for skiers leaving the slopes; either it is late in the day, or signs of bad weather are apparent, which only the foolhardy would ignore. Remember conditions can be as severe in the Scottish mountains in winter as they would be in the Alps abroad. The mountains can be dangerous to fools and kind to those who treat them with respect. The careless skier not only endangers his own life, he places in jeopardy the men of the Mountain Rescue Service, who so willingly go to the assistance of anyone in trouble. In cases of emergency, the Warden at the Shieling, or the Chairlift staff should first be notified.

PISTES

SUGAR BOWL

The best snow-holding area below 2,000 feet, situated just above the treeline. Usually skiable in the early part of the year, suitability can easily be checked as the ski road runs hard by the side of the slope. A useful downhill slope for the average skier, with plenty of space at the bottom for beginners. No permanent uphill locomotion, but on occasions a portable tow operates. STANDARD: BEGINNERS-AVERAGE.

LURCHER'S GULLY

Approximately one mile from the car park. Walking time average thirty minutes. Direction: From the middle of the car park, the Cairngorm chairlift station is on the immediate left and the entry to the car park on the immediate right. Walk straight ahead; it is the only long gully visible from this point. An excellent snow-holding slope skiable most of the season; length approximately one mile with a vertical rise of 1,100 feet. In a good snow year it can provide a run of almost two miles. No mechanisation. This run is not recommended for novices but can provide an excellent day's sport for the competent skier seeking solitude. STANDARD: COMPETENT.

LOWER COIRE CAS

This is the area spanned by the first section of the Cairngorm Chairlift, from the car park to the Shieling; it is particularly suitable for beginners, as is the whole Shieling area, when conditions are right. A trainer tow operates just below the Shieling and can be most helpful to those who have advanced beyond the awkward stage but are still not ready for steeper slopes. By travelling on the Chairlift to the Shieling station, suitable spots for practice can easily be noted, and on descent at the Shieling, the trainer tow is a few steps away. A good run can be had for the average skier from the Shieling to the car park when conditions are good. STANDARD: BEGINNERS TO AVERAGE. ACCENT BEGINNERS.

COIRE CAS

This is an exceedingly good snow-holding corrie, one of the most popular in the walking days before the advent of the Lifts and still exceedingly so in the early months of the year. Easily recognisable by looking up ahead over the first Chairlift Station to the right of the Shieling, a long magnificent sweep brooded over by the grandeur of the cornice on Fiacaill Ridge. The slope length measures 4,200 feet and is served by a T-bar tow covering 3,500 feet with a vertical rise of 789 feet. Near the top of the run the slopes are gentle and can provide an excellent training ground for beginners. As it descends, however, it steepens rapidly, with most of the gradient towards the end of the run. The piste, therefore, should only be used by a skier in full control of his movements. Descend at the Shieling station and the start of the T-bar tow is hard by. STANDARD: COMPETENT.

THE UPPER RUNS

For all the other major runs it is necessary to use the Cairngorm Chairlift for access, or alternatively walk up the mountainside until the vicinity of the top station on the shoulder of Cairngorm is reached. The use of the Chairlift is advisable; it gives extra ski-ing time and reliable information regarding weather and snow conditions can be had from the staff in passing, although it is not part of their job. Conditions and weather can be checked at the information desk in the Shieling.

WHITE LADY

This piste runs almost alongside the pylons of the Cairngorm Chairlift from the Shieling up to the top station, and prevailing conditions can be noted on the journey. A most popular run which can be entered from almost any place alongside the top station. In a poor snow year, or late in the season, it may be necessary to descend a short distance because of broken snow, but judicious erection of snow fences over the last few years has greatly increased the snow holding area. Slope length 3,600 feet, of which the Chairlift covers 3,468 feet with vertical rise of 1,056 feet.

Variation of approach and a much longer run can be had by way of the head of Coire na Ciste. With the pylons immediately left, ski downhill from the station, keeping to the left, and the approach is easily discernible and usually marked by poles. Another good variation can be had by branching off to the left of the main run approximately two-thirds of the way down. Coire Cas can then be entered at its highest gradient by turning right, and the run finished just below the Shieling Station. Care should be taken on entry to Coire Cas to avoid collision course with skiers using that piste. White Lady is a good fast piste, much favoured as the venue for races and skiable most of the season. Offers a variety of runs and should only be used by good controlled skiers. It can on occasions be icy. STANDARD: COMPETENT.

SNOW FENCE RUN

A comparitively new run made possible by the snow fences. An excellent traverse very suitable for beginners. It starts on the gentle slopes at the top of Coire na Ciste; just behind the top Station of

CAIRNGORM PLATEAU FROM CAIRNGORM TOP

the Chairlift. Easily descending, it wends its way left, round by the top of White Lady, under the pylons and so on across the face of the hill, with an easy descent to end in the gentle slopes at the top of Coire Cas. Snow conditions should be checked by novices before using this run, to avoid broken snow. STANDARD: BEGINNERS.

COIRE NA CISTE

One of the best ski runs in the area, a long steep sided gully topped by a large basin and easily accessible. On arrival at the Chairlift top station, bear left; after a few steps the corrie descends, gently at first sight, but appearances are deceptive and the lower reaches are steep. Excellent ski-ing available for the whole season and invariably usable in June. The steep sides of the corrie collect any drifting snow and the north-east exposure conserves it. The basin at the top provides excellent slopes for beginners and the spring snow is exceedingly good. The main piste has a slope of 6,800 feet or nearly a mile and one-third, with a vertical rise of 1,600 feet. While the first 4,000 feet at the top of the run can provide good sport for the average skier, the later stages are difficult and should only be attempted by the competent. A rope tow operates on part of the slope. Coire na Ciste is also a popular place for the holding of races. STANDARD—TOP BASIN: BEGINNERS. HIGHER PISTE: COMPETENT. LOWER SLOPE: VERY COMPETENT.

CISTE MHEAREAD

Walk almost straight ahead from the Chairlift Top Station with Coire na Ciste on the left and the summit of Cairngorm on the right; a few minutes in this direction ensures arrival at the top of Ciste Mhearead. A very pleasant sheltered corrie suitable for all classes of skier and guaranteed to catch every last blink of sunshine. Another excellent snow-holding area which can usually guarantee a run between 900 and 1.200 feet in June. The normal length, however is approximately 3,000 feet and good sport can be had all season although the spring snow is probably the best. In the interests of safety it would be wise to avoid ski-ing in this corrie, or any other, lying in the same general direction on this side of Cairngorm, should there be any likelihood of storm or mist. Well worth the short walk on a clear day. STANDARD: COMPETENT.

COIRE RAIBEIRT

Another good snow-holding corrie almost 5,000 feet long. Skirt the top of Ciste Mhearead on the left, keep Cairngorm on the immediate right, and a short walk should reach the top of Raibeirt. A steep slope useful to the fully independent skier only, and like Ciste

Mhearead recommended only in good clear weather. Like Lurchers Gully—a haven for the seeker of solitude. STANDARD: VERY COMPETENT.

FIACAILL OF COIRE CAS

Already mentioned under the familiar name of Fiacaill Ridge and described as being at the head of Coire Cas. The translation from the Gaelic means "The teeth of the steep corrie", and it is aptly named. The advanced skier can find two very good runs here, one coming off the north west slope of Cairngorm into Coire Cas and the other descending from the Fiacaill almost directly opposite on the other side, leading into the same corrie. Great care should be taken on these runs as considerable prowess is required for safe negotiation. STANDARD: EXPERT.

———————————

Donations towards the Cairngorms Winter Sports Development Appeal Fund may be sent to:

Cairngorms Winter Sports Development Board Ltd.,

47 High Street, Grantown-on-Spey.

GAELIC PLACE NAMES

Translated by J. M. BANNERMAN

Airgiod Meall	Hill of silver
Allt Ban	The white burn
Allt na Ciste	The burn of the box-shaped corrie
Allt Coire an t-Sneachda	The snow corrie burn
Allt Creag an Leth-choin	The burn of the lurcher's rocks
Allt na Doire	The burn of the grove
Allt Druidh	The burn of the shieling (*allt ruidh*)
Allt na Feithe Dhuibh	The black bog burn
Allt Mor	The big burn
Am Beanaidh	The burn of corners (*Beannach*) (?)
An t-Aonach	The expansive heath or moor
Allt nan Caber	The burn of trees
Aviemore	The great slope (*agaidh mor*)
Badaguish	The clump of pine trees
Ben Macdhui	The ben of the black pig (*Ben Muich Dhui*)
Braeriach	Brindled slope (*breach*)
Cadha Mor	The great wedge
Cairn Gorm	The blue cairn
Cairn Lochan	The cairn of the lochan
Cairn Toul	The cairn of the barn
Carn Eilrig	The cairn of the deer-walk
Clach Bharraig	The foundation stone
Cnap Coire na Spreidhe	The deer corrie lump (*cnap* pronounced "crap")
Coire Cas	The steep corrie
Coire na Ciste	Box-shaped corrie
Coire Laoigh Beg	The little corrie of the calves
Coire Laoigh Mor	The big corrie of the calves
Coire an Lochain	Corrie of the Lochan
Coire Raibeirt	Robert's corrie
Coire an t-Sneachda	The corrie of the snows
Coylumbridge	Bridge of the narrow leap
Craig Gowrie	Rock of the goats
Creag a' Chalamain	Rock of the pigeons (blue rock doves)
Craigellachie	Rock of Ellachie
Creag nan Gall	The rock of the Lowlanders (strangers)
Craeg Ghreusaiche	The rock of the cobbler
Craeg an Leth-choin	The rock of the lurcher
Creag Loisgte	The burnt rock

92

Creag Mheadhonach	The centre rock (pronounded "craig vean")
Creagan Gorm	The blue rocks
Fiacaill a Choire Chais	The teeth of the steep corrie
Feith Bhuidhe	The yellow bog
Garbh Allt	The rough burn
Garbh Uisge	The rough water
Glen More	The big glen
Inverdruie	The banks of the river Druie
Lairig Ghru	Possibly the forbidding or gloomy pass (from *gruamach*)
Lairig an Laoigh	Pass of the calves
Loch Avon	Loch of the river (pronouncee "A'an")
Loch a Gharbh Choire	The loch of the rough corrie
Loch an Eilein	The loch of the island
Loch Etchachan	Loch of the junipers (*aitonnach*)
Loch Morlich	The loch of the great sloping hillside (*leacann*) (?)
Lochan na Beinne	The lochan of the ben
Lochan Buidhe	The yellow lochan
Lochan Dubh a Chadha	The black lochan of the wedge-shaped hill
Lochan nan Geadas	Lochan of the pike
Lochan nan Nathrach	Lochan of the adders
An Lochan Uaine	The green lochan
Meall a' Bhuachaille	The hill of the herdsman
Mam Suim	The rounded knoll
Monadh Liath	The grey hills
River Luineag	The surging river
Rothiemurchus	*Ràth á mhór ghuithais:* The plain of the great pines
Ryvoan	The bothy shieling (*airidh bhoan*)
Sluggan	The gullet
Sron an Aonaich	The point of the expansive moor or heath
Stac an Fharaidh	The pinnacle of observation
Stac na h-Iolaire	The rock of the eagles

Note.—As guides to pronunciation: The letter *h* softens other consonants which precede it. *ch* and *gh* followed by a vowel are pronounced *h*; otherwise they are guttural. Initial *bh* becomes *v*; so does *mh*. Medial and final *bh*, *dh* and *th* are scarcely pronounced; they merely lengthen the preceding vowel.

BOOKS
ON THE CAIRNGORMS
AND STRATH SPEY

Alexander, H.	*The Cairngorms* (1928)
Hill Burton, J.	*Cairngorm Mountains* (1864)
Cairngorm Club	*Journal*
Cassillis, Earl of	*Rulers of Strathspey* (1911)
Darling, Fraser and Boyd, J. M.	*Natural History in the Highlands and Islands* (1964) Collins
Eyre-Todd, G.	*Speyside from the Moray Firth to the Cairngorms* (1908)
Firsoff, V. A.	*The Cairngorms on Foot and Ski* (1949)
,, ,,	*In the Hills of Breadalbane* (1954)
Forsyth, W.	*In the Shadow of the Cairngorms* (1900)
'Glenmore'	*Highland Legends* (1789)
Gordon, Seton	*The Cairngorm Hills* (1925)
,, ,,	*Highways and Byways in the Central Highlands* (1948) Macmillan, 10s. 6d.
Grant, Mrs. A.	*Superstitions of the Highlands* (1811)
Grant, Miss E. (Mrs. Smith of Baltiboys)	*Memoirs of a Highland Lady* (1898) (A very interesting and well-written account of rural life in the early nineteenth century)
Grant, Miss I. F.	*Everyday Life on an Old Highland Farm* (1926)
Haldane, J. R. B.	*Drove Roads of Scotland* (1952)
Harvie-Brown, J. A. and Buckley, T. E.	*A Vertebrate Fauna of the Moray Basin* (1895) Douglas, Edinburgh, 2 Vols.
Holmes, W. K.	*Tramping Scottish Hills* (1947)
Inglis, H. R. G.	*Hill Path Contours* (1933) Gall & Inglis, Edinburgh
,, ,,	*Walks Round Carr Bridge* Carr Bridge Amenities Association
,, ,,	*Romantic Badenoch* (1925). Johnstone, Kingussie
Lauder, Sir T. Dick	*The Wolf of Badenoch* (1827)
,, ,, ,,	*An Account of the Great Floods of the Province of Moray* (1836)
Lees, J. C.	*History of the County of Inverness* (1897)
Loader, Catherine M.	*Cairngorm Adventure at Glenmore Lodge.* A book about the Scottish Centre of Outdoor Training. Wm. Brown, Edinburgh (1952)
Macbain, A.	*Place Names of Inverness-shire* (1899)

McCrow, Brenda	*From Braemar to Speyside* Oliver & Boyd, Edinburgh
Mackintosh, C. Fraser	*Antiquarian Notes* (1897)
Mackintosh, H. B.	*Pilgrimages in Moray* (1924). Elgin
MacMillan, H.	*Rothiemurchus* (1907)
Macpherson, A.	*Glimpses of Church and Social Life in the Highlands in Olden Times* (1893)
Mearns, S. N.	*Around Strathspey* (1948), Mearns, Aberdeen, 2s. 6d. (An interesting illustrated guide to the Aviemore district)
Mitchell, Sir A.	*Vacation Notes in Strathspey*
Murray, W. H.	*Mountaineering in Scotland* (1947) (One chapter on the Cairngorm)
Perry, Richard	*In the High Grampians* (1948). Lindsay Drummond,
Plumb, Charles	*Walking in the Grampians*
Poucher, W. A.	*A Camera in the Cairngorms* (1947)
Robertson, J. R.	*General View of the Agriculture of the County of Inverness* (1808)
Salmond, J. B.	*Wade in Scotland* (1938)
Scottish Mountaineering Club	*Cairngorm Guide*, Vol. I: Cairngorms (10s. 6d.)
Scottish Youth Hostels Association	*Cairngorms, Deeside and Angus Glens*. A Hosteller's Guide, 1961 (2s. 4d. post free from S.Y.H.A.)
Sinton, T.	*By Loch and River, Memoirs of Loch Laggan and Upper Spey* *The Poetry of Badenoch* (1906)
Shaw, L.	*History of the Province of Moray* (1882)
Steven, H. M. and Carlyle, A.	*The Native Pinewoods of Scotland*. Oliver & Boyd, Edinburgh, 1959
Stewart, W. Grant	*Lectures on the Mountains* (1866)
Thornton, W. P. T.	*A Sporting Tour through the Northern Parts of England and great parts of the Highlands of Scotland* (reprinted Sportsman Library)
Wood, Wendy	*The Secret of Spey* (1930)

ON THE SLUGGAN TRACK
The view extends north-west across Strath Spey to the Monadh Liath

APPROACHES TO THE PARK

ACCESS ROAD

The majority of visitors, whether they travel by car, cycle, or afoot, approach Glen More by the one road from Aviemore.

The route from Aviemore leaves the main north road (A. 9) about 300 yards south of Aviemore Station, and is signposted "Rothiemurchus and Glenmore, B. 970". Follow this for two miles until a stone bridge is reached at the hamlet of Coylumbridge. Ignore the left-hand road here, and turn half right up a good tarred road which winds through pinewoods to Loch Morlich.

There are two small car parks suitable as picnic points, beside the Loch; one is near the western end, the other just past the further, eastern end.

Just beyond the end of the loch the road forks. The right-hand fork leads in turn to the camp sites, the Norwegian Huts, the Ski

Road (see p. 106) and the new Glenmore Lodge of the Scottish Council for Physical Recreation. The left fork leads only to the Loch Morlich Youth Hostel, and the Forest Offices.

Distances from Aviemore are: Loch Morlich, 5 miles; Youth Hostel and Camp Site, 7 miles; New Glenmore Lodge, 7½ miles.

BY ROAD

Aviemore, which is 148 miles from Edinburgh, 145 miles from Glasgow, 83 miles from Perth and 31 miles from Inverness, is centrally placed as regards the main highways through the Central Highlands. First-class roads run northwards to Inverness, Grantown, and north-eastern Scotland; southwards to Pitlochry, Perth, and the Lowlands; and westwards to Fort William. The cyclist will find their gradients easier than the height of the land might suggest.

BY RAIL

Aviemore has a station on the main line from Perth and the South to Inverness and the North, and express trains stop there. The journey from Edinburgh or Glasgow takes 4 or 5 hours; that from London about 11 hours.

At certain times, particularly in the ski-ing season, excursion tickets are issued from Glasgow, Edinburgh, Perth, and other distant towns which allow the holder to spend a holiday in the district at a considerably reduced cost. Details are available from British Railways who issue a brochure entitled: *Ski-ing in Scotland*.

HIRED CARS

The nearest point to the Park at which cars may be hired is Aviemore, distant 7 miles from Glen More Camp Site.

CARS BY RAIL

During the holiday season, British Railways carry cars to the Scottish Highlands, to points convenient for reaching Glen More, by the following services: London-Perth, London-Stirling, Birmingham (Sutton Coldfield)-Stirling, York-Newcastle-Inverness.

MOTOR BUSES

LOCAL SERVICES. At the time we go to press there are NO all-the-year-round daily services in the vicinity of Glenmore that would enable a visitor to reach the camp site, or to make local journeys therefrom.

During July and August, on Wednesdays, Saturdays and Sundays only, a service is operated between Aviemore and the Glenmore

Camp Site. Timetables, price 2d. (or 5d. post free) may be obtained from: Norman Smith, The Garage, Grange Road, Grantown-on-Spey.

LONG-DISTANCE SERVICES. During the summer months, from mid-June to mid-September only, two services link Aviemore (but not Glenmore) with places to the north and south. One of these is the Glasgow-Perth-Aviemore-Inverness-Elgin service run by Messrs. Alexanders (Midland) Ltd. of Camelon, Falkirk. The other is the Edinburgh-Perth-Aviemore-Inverness service of Scottish Omnibuses Ltd., St. Andrew Square, Edinburgh. Details may be obtained from the respective companies.

AIR SERVICES

The nearest airport is at Inverness, 32 miles away. There are regular daily flights to Glasgow and London.

ON FOOT

Besides the road routes described above, the Park may be reached by several hill paths, certain of which involve a very long tramp from the starting point; the more important paths are described here.

THE SLUGGAN PASS. This is the shortest route from Boat of Garten. A gravelled track leaves the public road just 4 miles from both Boat of Garten and Coylumbridge and climbs steadily uphill for one mile—giving lovely views over Strath Spey, and then descends gently for two miles to Loch Morlich. Turn left for the Camp Site, one mile on.

FROM NETHYBRIDGE VIA RYVOAN. The road running east, on the south bank of the river Nethy, leads to Forest Lodge, from which point a track, which is a right of way for walkers only, continues southwards to enter the Park through the Ryvoan Pass, and so down to Glen More, the total distance being 10 miles from Nethybridge.

FROM KINCRAIG. A secondary road runs eastward to Feshiebridge, where some fine cataracts and rock pools may be seen. Beyond the bridge the left-hand road continues northwards past the Forestry Commission property of Inshriach to South Kinrara. Beyond those plantations a well-trodden footpath diverges on the right to climb between two small hills to pine-embowered Loch an Eilein. Bearing left up the loch's western shore, a right-hand turn at the northern end (signposted, "Lairig Ghru" and "Allt Druidh"), followed by a left-fork half a mile further on, brings one on to a track which runs eastwards to the main Lairig Ghru approach path; there turn left and follow that path north to Coylumbridge, whence the right-hand road beyond the bridge runs to Glen More Camp Site. A very pleasant walk of some 15 miles, through forests the whole way; this route avoids most of the tarmac and affords wonderful views of the Speyside hills.

FROM BOAT OF GARTEN one may work eastwards on by-roads through the Forest of Abernethy to Forest Lodge, thence southwards through Ryvoan Pass. This route of about 13 miles is an interesting alternative to the shorter 9-mile approach by the Sluggan Pass road.

FROM BRAEMAR, the easiest of the three possible routes is the Lairig an Laoigh, or Calves Pass, an ancient right of way which runs northwards up the Derry Burn from Derry Lodge in Glen Lui, passes to the east of Loch Avon and Bynack More, and then works round to the Ryvoan Pass and so to Glen More Camp Site. The distance to that point from Braemar is about 26 miles.

The alternative is the famous Lairig Ghru route, a strenuous walk of some 28 miles, involving a climb to 2,733 feet above sea-level at the summit of the pass, and requiring some 12 hours for its comple-

SCHOOLGIRLS FROM GLASGOW OFF TO THEIR FIRST
SKI-ING LESSON

tion. After entering Rothiemurchus Forest, the path for Glen More diverges eastward from the Aviemore route, as described in the chapter on hill walks. During the winter months—and indeed well on into late spring—the Lairig Ghru is normally snowbound.

For the seasoned, experienced walker, a fine high level approach is that up Glen Derry to Coire Etchachan, thence north to the Shelter Stone beside Loch Avon. The Feith Buidhe is then crossed and an ascent made to the saddle south-west of the Cairn Gorm summit. From that point there is an easy descent via Coire Cas to the main Cairn Gorm path and so to Glen More Camp Site.

FROM BLAIR ATHOLL, it is possible to reach the Lairig Ghru route at White Bridge across the Dee by way of Glen Tilt, but the total distance of some 36 miles makes an overnight encampment *en route* essential for all but the fittest of walkers.

FROM TOMINTOUL, there is a fine hill track some 22 miles long, via Bridge of Brown, Dorback Lodge, the Eag Mhor gap, Loch a' Chnuic, and the Ryvoan Pass. This is well shown on the one-inch Ordnance maps of the Cairngorms. It involves fording several streams. A longer alternative route ascends the river Avon to link up with the Lairig an Laoigh.

GENERAL INFORMATION

CAMPING GROUNDS

MAIN CAMP

A public camping ground has been opened at the eastern end of Loch Morlich, occupying a pleasant open site below the slopes of the Cairn Gorm. The facilities include water supply, lavatories, and a room for shelter and recreation in wet weather. The current charges, liable to revision, are:

Per tent of normal size .. .. 1s. 6d. per night
10s. per week

Per motor cycle and tent .. .. 3s. per night
18s. per week

Per car and caravan or car and tent .. .. .. 6s. per night; 36s. per week

Bookings are not arranged in advance, permits being issued at the Camp. Inquiries should be addressed to:

The Conservator of Forests for North Scotland,
Forestry Commission,
60 Church Street,
Inverness.

JUVENILE CAMP

A separate Camping Area is reserved for the exclusive use of Juvenile Organisations and for this area advance bookings must be arranged. No charges are made. Inquiries should be addressed to:

The Conservator of Forests for North Scotland,
60 Church Street,
Inverness.

It should be noted that no arrangements for *free* camping can be made at the Park itself.

NORWEGIAN HUTS

At Glen More the "Norwegian" huts are reserved for Youth Organisations, including schools, colleges and universities. These huts consist of one building, comprising two large huts with a communicating apartment. One hut is partitioned into four rooms, used as sleeping quarters. There are no bunks in the sleeping quarters. The other hut is divided into three—cookhouse, office or store, and dining-room-cum-common-room. The communicating apartment contains sprays, washhand basins and lavatories. There is a drying room and a hot water system, but fuel, cooking utensils, beds and bedding are not provided. About 40 can be accommodated in the huts. The following is the scale of charges for Junior Organisations:

    £8 per 2-week period   £4 per 1-week period

    £5 per 3-week period   £3 per week-end period

    Senior Organisations pay £9 per week.

Applications for the use of the huts should be addressed to: The Conservator of Forests for North Scotland, 60 Church Street, Inverness.

PARKING GROUNDS

There are two low-level car parks. One is at the eastern end of Loch Morlich, an excellent spot for a picnic. The other is opposite the camp site. There are no charges. There is also a County Council car park (with parking fees) at the head of the Ski Road.

THE CAMP SHOP

A shop, operated by an independent shopkeeper, is now open all the year round at the camp site. The goods stocked include bread, milk, tinned provisions, paraffin and postage stamps. There is a small tea-room attached, and in summer a sub-post office is operated.

VANS

Travelling vans, selling provisions and general household goods, call at the camp site on several days each week, usually on Tuesdays, Thursdays and Saturdays.

THE RECREATION ROOM AND CHURCH

A large room close to the camp site is open to campers as a wet weather shelter, and for recreation.

Adjoining this room is a Sanctuary which has been dedicated for religious purposes by the Church of Scotland. Services of an inter-denominational character are held there on Sunday evenings throughout the year, and are open to all people interested.

THE DEER FENCES

The plantations of the Glen More Forest Park are protected from the red deer that roam the hills by a six-foot high fence, and this must be crossed in order to gain access to the hills. Gates, stiles or cattle grids have been provided at the principal points likely to be used by walkers, and in particular on the following routes: Main Road to Aviemore, Sluggan Pass, Footpath to Meall a' Bhuacaille,

Ryvoan Path, Allt Ban Path, Ski Road, path towards Rothiemurchus and south-east corner of Loch Morlich. All gates must be
closed after use, and only in an emergency should the fence be
crossed at any other point.

THE CAIRNGORM HILL RACE

Once a year, usually on the third Saturday in July, a race is held
from the Old Glenmore Lodge to the summit of the Cairngorm and
back. The present (1965) record for the 3,000-foot climb and descent
is 73 minutes. The race, which is held under the rules of the North of
Scotland Amateur Athletic Association, is open to all comers, and
entries may be sent to the Secretary, Cairngorm Race, Glenmore.

FOREST OFFICES

The Forester in charge of Glen More Forest Park has an office
behind the Youth Hostel, and any enquiries concerning the woodlands may be made there.

The Camp Warden's office, where tickets for camping are issued,
is close to the camp site.

LETTERBOX AND PHONE

There is a letterbox with a once-daily collection, close to the Youth
Hostel. Also a public telephone kiosk.

YOUTH HOSTELS

The old Glenmore Lodge is now a large Youth Hostel named *Loch
Morlich*, after the loch beside which it stands, and to avoid con-
fusion with the new Glenmore Lodge of the Scottish Council for
Physical Recreation.

SKI-ING IN COIRE CAS

THE SNOW-CLAD CAIRNGORMS SEEN FROM GLEN MORE LODGE

The next nearest hostel is at Aviemore, 7 miles from the Loch Morlich Hostel, but during busy seasons prior booking is desirable there. The large hostel at Kingussie, 17 miles from the Park, is also a convenient centre if cycles, trains, or buses are used to lessen the walking distance.

Other hostels are situated at Tomintoul (22 miles), Inverey near Braemar (23 miles), and Braemar (28 miles); the distances are those by hill tracks in each case.

Further information will be found in the Scottish Youth Hostels Association Handbook obtainable from the Association at 7 Bruntsfield Crescent, Edinburgh, 10, price 1s. (1s. 4d. post free).

HOTELS

Hotels within walking distance of the Park are:

At Aviemore: Cairngorm, Lynwilg, Alt-na-Craig, Craigellachie House, Dell, Ravenscraig, Aviemore Motel, High Range, Speyside and Alltnacriche.

At Boat of Garten: The Boat and Craigard.

Other centres, from which the Park may be reached by the aid of car or cycle, are: Carrbridge, Nethybridge, Grantown, Kingussie, Newtonmore, Kincraig and Tomintoul.

New hotels are planned at Aviemore and Coylumbridge, to be opened in 1966.

MOUNTAIN RESCUE

There is a First Aid Post and a Mountain Rescue Post at the White Lady Shieling. Anyone in need of help should contact the Forester ('phone Aviemore 271, or the Inverness-shire Police, Aviemore 222.) A Mountain Rescue team has been formed).

MISCELLANEOUS

Among the groups of people who regularly use the Forest Park for training purposes are the Royal Air Force Mountain Rescue Squad, from Kinloss, and the Outward Bound School at Burghead, Morayshire.

Though there are no facilities for hiring ponies at the Park, Speyside as a whole is a well-known pony-trekking centre, and there are riding stables at Aviemore and Newtonmore.

FOREST ROADS

Only two roads within the Forest Park are open to cars and similar vehicles, namely:

(1) The main tarred road in from Coylumbridge to the Youth Hostel and the new Glenmore Lodge.

(2) The Ski Road up the north slope of the Cairn Gorm.

The remaining roads within the Park are Forest Roads, and are closed to general wheeled traffic. Except at times of exceptional fire hazard, however, all the Forest Roads are freely open to *walkers*.

MAPS

All the Park and the neighbouring areas of the Grampian Mountains, including the Cairngorms National Nature Reserve, are shown on the Ordnance Survey *Tourist Map of the Cairngorms*, one-inch to the mile scale; price 15s. 0d. This is both practical and beautiful, with full contour colouring.

Nine-tenths of the Forest Park, from Loch Morlich and the Lairig Ghru eastwards, is shown on the Ordnance Survey One-inch Sheet No. 38 entitled "Grantown and Cairngorm".

The approaches to the Forest Park from Aviemore, and most of the adjacent Rothiemurchus Forest, appear on Ordnance Survey One-inch Sheet No. 37, entitled "Kingussie".

AN LOCHAN VAINE—THE GREEN LOCHAN AT RYVOAN

In Messrs. Bartholmew's Half-inch Series, the whole of the Park appears on Sheet No. 51, entitled "The Grampians".

THE SKI ROAD

Until 1959 the nearest public highway to Glen More was that at Coylumbridge, five miles from Glen More Lodge. In that year the Inverness-shire County Council, aided by a substantial grant from the Forestry Commission, took over the former private road as far as Glen More Lodge, and extended it well up into the hills.

This is now known as the Ski Road, and to reach it from Aviemore you go two miles east to Coylumbridge and proceed straight on through the outskirts of Rothiemurchus Forest to Glen More Forest and Loch Morlich. Bear right at the first fork beyond the Loch, then right again at the next fork. The road climbs steadily up through the pinewoods, then out on to the open braes by a series of hairpin bends.

At the top, where there is a turning point and a car park, the road reaches a height of 2,000 feet. A wonderful view opens out to the north, right over Loch Morlich to the far Monadhliath Hills. The White Shieling shelter and restaurant lies a quarter of a mile farther on up the brae, and may be reached either on foot or by the Chair Lift. Ahead you can see far into the Corries, with their ski-runs and rock climbs.

The daily charges laid down by the County Council at the Car Park at the head of the road are currently (1965) as follows:

Winter Ski-ing Season *1st November to 30th April*		*Other times of year* *1st May to 31st October*
Cars	3s. od.	1s. 6d.
Motor cycles	1s. od.	6d.
Motor caravans & Minibuses	4s. od.	2s. od.

Other rates are prescribed for larger vehicles such as coaches and lorries.

THE WHITE LADY SHIELING

This is a shelter and restaurant situated about 500 yards above the top of the Ski Road, adjacent to the Chairlift and close to the White Lady Ski Run. Visitors using the Chairlift should alight at the Middle Station. It is owned by the Cairngorm Trust, and was built in 1962 with the aid of public subscriptions and an anonymous donation of £20,000. Its object is to provide shelter for all who walk, climb, or ski in the Cairngorms. A resident warden is in charge.

Here you will find heated shelter, a restaurant providing hot drinks and snacks for 200 people, toilet facilities, a public telephone, and a shop which sells postcards and maps. Outside, an alpine garden features many of the rarer plants of the hills.

Most important, the White Lady Shieling houses a Mountain Rescue Post, where first-aid equipment of every kind is always available. The staff and volunteer helpers are trained to cope with every emergency, from minor mishaps to a major expedition into the wintry hills to bring in a casualty.

OTHER REFRESHMENT FACILITIES AT THE SKI-ING GROUNDS

There is a tea-room, close to the Car Park, just at the foot of the Chairlift's lower section. Also a small refreshment stand at the very top of the upper section of the Chairlift.

THE CHAIRLIFT

The Cairngorm Chairlift was first opened in 1962 by the Cairngorms Winter Sports Development Board Ltd.; it cost nearly £40,000 and was built with the aid of public subscriptions. As since extended, it now runs from the Car Park at the top of the Ski Road, past the White Lady Shieling (where there is an intermediate stop) to the shoulder of The Cairngorm. It is 1,156 yards (¾ of a mile) long, and rises 1,000 feet (from 2,500 to 3,500 feet above sea level).

It gives access in winter to the largest and highest snowfields in Britain, as well as to the widest expanse of open mountain country for ramblers. It operates for about 11 months of the year—normally from early December to late October—throughout the daylight hours, seven days a week. From the top station the walk to the summit of The Cairngorm, 4,084 feet, can be done in from 15 to 30 minutes, according to the fitness of the walker.

Only very adverse weather conditions, such as high wind, halt the Lift; otherwise it operates according to demand, and can carry up to 500 persons per hour.

THE SKI TOWS

A the present time (early 1965) two Ski Tows are in operation, both near the Chairlift and the White Lady Shieling. Others are planned for future development, including one in the Coire na Ciste.

CHARGES AND DETAILS OF CHAIRLIFT AND SKI TOW

The following information has kindly been provided by the Manager, Mr. R. Clyde. The charges are those in force in 1965, and readers should appreciate that they may be varied from time to time.

CHARGES ON CAIRNGORM CHAIRLIFT
WINTER FARES

1.	Return ticket "all the way"	6/-
2.	Return either section	4/-
3.	Single each section	3/-
4.	Single, all the way	5/-

Books of 8 tickets—£1—one ticket per Chairlift Section and Coire Cas Tow.

Day Card—unlimited use of any machine £1 5s. od.

A refund system will operate on the day cards in the event of the tows being closed by bad weather.

Return ticket   10/- Complete journey
Return ticket   5/- each section
Single ticket   5/- Complete journey
                        3/- each section

CHARGES ON SKI-TOWS (Winter only)

3/- per trip, unless paid for by a Book Ticket or Day Card as explained above.

CAIRNGORM CHAIRLIFT

An automatic two-seater chairlift capable of carrying 600 persons per hour over a total length of 6,033 feet (1·14 miles) and a vertical lift of 1,425 feet. The lift is in two stages (1) Car Park Section, 2,565 feet long with vertical lift of 369 feet and (2) White Lady Section, 3,468 feet long and vertical rise of 1,056 feet. Passengers may travel right through or off/on at Middle Station.

COIRE CAS SKI TOW

A T-bar tow capable of carrying 600 persons per hour over 3,500 feet and a vertical lift of 789 feet.

SHIELING TRAINER TOW

A T-bar Tow capable of carrying 600 persons per hour, 1,000 feet long with a vertical lift of 180 feet.

LET THEM KNOW ....

WHERE YOU GO ....

Visitors who set out on long excursions to the higher hills are asked to heed the following notice which they will see displayed beside "posting boxes" at the main starting points of recognised paths.

POLICE NOTICE:
Everyone going climbing or walking in the Cairngorms is specially requested to leave a notice in the box stating:
Intended route and time of return
Name and Address
Registration number of car left in park or vicinity
This information could save your life.

As an instance of the difficulties facing rescuers, the remote country beyond the Cairngorm was formerly "dead ground" for the radio sets used by the Mountain Rescue Group. A special transmitter has been set up on the Cairngorm summit to overcome this problem.

SCOTTISH SPORTS HOLIDAYS

Two booklets describing current arrangements can be obtained free of charge from The Scottish Tourist Board, of 2 Rutland Place, West End, Edinburgh 1, and 2 Academy Street, Inverness.

One, entitled *Scottish Sports Holidays*, gives details of Pony Trekking, Horse Riding, Mountaineering, Fishing and Golf; all from organised centres in the district. The other, entitled *Winter Sports in Scotland*, gives details of Ski-ing Schools and hotels with winter sports facilities on Speyside.

BATHING

The safest and best bathing is at the east end of Loch Morlich where, at the nearest point to the Camp Site, there is a dry, sandy shore. All bathers, especially non-swimmers, should be very careful as there are deep hollows in the bed of the loch; and no children should bathe unaccompanied by adults.

BOATING AND FISHING

Coarse fishing is available on Loch Morlich and permits may be had from the Camp Shop. The charge for the use of the boat, whether for fishing or just for rowing, is 2s. per hour. Fishing from the banks of Loch Morlich is permitted at a charge of 3s. per day for adults, 1s. 6d. per day for children. Weekly tickets: 12s. 6d. for adults; 6s. for children.

Fishing and boating may also be enjoyed at reasonable charges on the waters of the neighbouring estate of Rothiemurchus; inquiries may be made at Aviemore Post Office. Salmon are found in the Spey, and trout in most of the lochs.

LOCH MORLICH IN WINTER, LOOKING TOWARDS COIRE CAS

THE CAIRNGORMS NATURE RESERVE

Contributed By THE NATURE CONSERVANCY

The Cairngorms Nature Reserve which lies south of Glen More, covers 39,689 acres (16,068 ha.) and is by far the largest in Britain and one of the largest in Europe. It ranges from 840 ft. (260 m.) in altitude at Loch-an-Eilein, and 1,400 ft. (426 m.) at Derry Lodge, to 4,296 ft. (1,309 m.) on Ben Macdhui. It extends over much of one of the largest areas of high ground in Scotland and includes the summits of Braeriach and Cairn Toul, both over 4,000 ft. (1,218 m.).

Its chief scientific interests lie, firstly, in the subarctic summit plateau with its distinctive arctic-alpine plant and animal communities which have remained entirely, or almost entirely, untouched by human influence and, secondly, in the largest surviving areas of the ancient Caledonian Forest, parts of which are still self-regenerating and contain their naturally associated flora and fauna.

There is a great variety of plant communities, mainly because of the wide range of altitude from the pine and birch woods upwards over the open moors to the corries and exposed summits. Over two hundred species of flowering plants, and several hundred species of ferns, mosses, litchens, fungi, etc., are found on the Reserve.

In the great corries there are many arctic-alpine and sub-arctic species, including some of the rarest members of the British flora, such as the brook saxifrage (*Saxifraga rivularis*), the alpine pearlwort (*Sagina saginoides*), wavy meadow grass (*Poa flexuosa*) and alpine hare's-foot sedge (*Carex lachenalii*).

On the exposed high summits the vegetation is of special interest because of the severe weather conditions prevailing at such altitudes. Among the flowering plants present, along with mosses and lichens, on such windswept areas are the moss campion (*Silene acaulis*), the least willow (*Salix herbacea*), the rigid sedge (*Carex bigelowii*), the trifid rush (*Juncus trifidulus*) and the curved woodrush (*Luzula arcuata*).

The mammals and birds of the Reserve are of exceptional interest; all the main species are described in the chapter on Wild Life in this Guide.

The invertebrate fauna of the region is of great interest and still inadequately known, particularly the insects of the highest tops which are peculiarly adapted to their windswept environment.

The Nature Conservancy maintains its Speyside Research Station at Achantoul, Aviemore.

THE SPLENDID CALEDONIAN PINES AROUND LOCH AN EILEIN, IN ROTHIEMURCHUS FOREST

FORESTRY COMMISSION GUIDES

Available from Her Majesty's Stationery Office at
the addresses on back cover

ARGYLL 4s. (4s. 7d.)

QUEEN ELIZABETH FOREST
PARK (Ben Lomond,
Loch Ard, Trossachs),
3s. 7d. (4s. 1d.)

BEDGEBURY PINETUM
(Kent) 3s. 6d.
(4s.)

CAMBRIAN FORESTS 5s.
(5s. 7d.)

SNOWDONIA FOREST
PARK 5s. (5s. 6d.)

FOREST OF DEANS 6s.
(6s. 6d.)

NEW FOREST 5s. (5s. 7d.)

GLEN TROOL 6s. (6s. 7d.)

THE BORDER FOREST
PARK 5s. (5s. 7d.)

Prices in brackets include postage

*A list of booklets, bulletins, reports, leaflets, and other
publications dealing with the more technical aspects of
forestry, and the free pamphlets* Forestry in Scotland,
Britain's New Forests, and Camping in the Forest
Parks, *will be sent on request by:*

FORESTRY COMMISSION
25 SAVILE ROW
LONDON, W.1

Printed in Scotland by Her Majesty's Stationery Office Press, Edinburgh
Wt. 72984 K72 (3034)

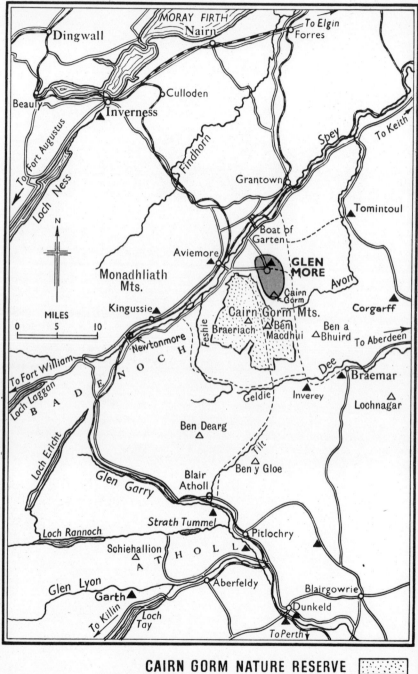

CAIRN GORM NATURE RESERVE

The Youth Hostel at Glen More is called "Loch Morlich"

MAPS OF THE
GLEN MORE FOREST PARK

The main map is on a scale of $5/6$ inch to
1 mile. (approx.) and has the following legend:

Forest Park, plantable land . . . . ▭

,, ,, unplantable land . . . . ▭

Land over 2,000 feet above sea level . ▭

,, ,, 3,000 ,, ,, ,, ,, ▭

Footpaths - - - - - - - - - - Roads ═══════

Rivers ～～～～～ Railways ▬▬▬▬▬

County Boundaries —·—·—·—·—

Cliffs and Crags ～～～～～～

The smaller map, on a scale of about 12
miles to one inch, shows the approaches to the
area.

Youth Hostels are shown -thus : ▲

Principal summits thus : △

© *Crown copyright* 1966

Published by
HER MAJESTY'S STATIONERY OFFICE

To be purchased from
13A Castle Street, Edinburgh 2
49 High Holborn, London w.c.1
423 Oxford Street, London w.1
109 St. Mary Street, Cardiff
Brazennose Street, Manchester 2
50 Fairfax Street, Bristol 1
35 Smallbrook, Ringway, Birmingham 5
80 Chichester Street, Belfast 1
or through any bookseller
and at the Camp Shop, Glen More